Catherine Cookson was born in Tyne Dock and the place of her birth provides the background she so vividly creates in many of her novels. Although acclaimed as a regional writer – her novel THE ROUND TOWER won the Winifred Holtby Award for the best regional novel of 1968 – her readership spreads throughout the world. Her work has been translated into more than a dozen languages and Corgi alone has sold almost 40,000,000 copies of her novels, including those written under the name of Catherine Marchant.

Mrs Cookson was born the illegitimate daughter of a poverty-stricken woman, Kate, whom she believed to be her older sister. Catherine began work in service but eventually moved south to Hastings where she met and married a local grammar school master. At the age of forty she began writing with great success about the lives of the working class people of the North-East with whom she had grown up, including her intriguing autobiography, OUR KATE. Her many bestselling novels have established her as one of the most popular of contemporary women novelists.

Mrs Cookson now lives in Northumberland.

Other Books by Catherine Cookson

THE GARMENT
SLINKY JANE
HANNAH MASSEY
THE IRON FACADE
THE SLOW AWAKENING
MISS MARTHA MARY
  CRAWFORD
THE INVISIBLE CORD
THE GAMBLING MAN
THE TIDE OF LIFE
THE GIRL
THE MAN WHO CRIED
THE CINDER PATH
THE WHIP
HAMILTON
THE BLACK VELVET GOWN
GOODBYE HAMILTON
A DINNER OF HERBS
HAROLD
THE MOTH
THE PARSON'S DAUGHTER
THE CULTURED
  HANDMAIDEN
THE HARROGATE SECRET
THE BLACK CANDLE

and published by Corgi Books

The Mallen Trilogy
THE MALLEN STREAK
THE MALLEN GIRL
THE MALLEN LITTER

The Tilly Trotter Trilogy
TILLY TROTTER
TILLY TROTTER WED
TILLY TROTTER WIDOWED

The Bill Bailey Trilogy
BILL BAILEY
BILL BAILEY'S LOT
BILL BAILEY'S DAUGHTER

For Children
OUR JOHN WILLIE
MRS FLANNAGAN'S TRUMPET
MATTY DOOLIN
GO TELL IT TO MRS
  GOLIGHTLY
JOE AND THE GLADIATOR
LANKY JONES

Autobiography
CATHERINE COOKSON
  COUNTRY

*   *   *   *

KATE HANNIGAN
THE FIFTEEN STREETS
COLOUR BLIND
MAGGIE ROWAN
ROONEY
THE MENAGERIE
FANNY McBRIDE
FENWICK HOUSES
THE BLIND MILLER
THE LONG CORRIDOR
THE UNBAITED TRAP
KATIE MULHOLLAND
THE ROUND TOWER
THE NICE BLOKE
THE GLASS VIRGIN
THE INVITATION
THE DWELLING PLACE
FEATHERS IN THE FIRE
PURE AS THE LILY

The Mary Ann Novels
A GRAND MAN
THE LORD AND MARY ANN
THE DEVIL AND MARY ANN
LOVE AND MARY ANN
LIFE AND MARY ANN
MARRIAGE AND MARY ANN
MARY ANN'S ANGELS
MARY ANN AND BILL

Writing as Catherine Marchant
HOUSE OF MEN
THE FEN TIGER
HERITAGE OF FOLLY

Autobiography
OUR KATE

CATHERINE COOKSON

LET ME MAKE MYSELF PLAIN

A Personal Anthology

CORGI BOOKS

LET ME MAKE MYSELF PLAIN: A PERSONAL ANTHOLOGY

A CORGI BOOK   0 552 13407 4

Originally published in Great Britain by
Bantam Press, a division of Transworld Publishers Ltd.

PRINTING HISTORY
Bantam Press edition published 1988
Corgi edition published 1990

This book is set in 10/11pt Linotron 202 Bembo by
Rowland Phototypesetting Ltd., Bury St Edmunds, Suffolk

Corgi Books are published by Transworld Publishers Ltd.,
61–63 Uxbridge Road, Ealing, London W5 5SA, in Australia by
Transworld Publishers (Australia) Pty. Ltd., 15–23 Helles Avenue,
Moorebank, NSW 2170, and in New Zealand by Transworld
Publishers (N.Z.) Ltd., Cnr. Moselle and Waipareira Avenues,
Henderson, Auckland.

Made and printed in Great Britain by
Cox and Wyman Ltd., Reading, Berks.

To
Canon George Chadwick of Corbridge
and Father Tom Power of Haydon Bridge,
two good men with whom I have had many
helpful discussions

CONTENTS

AUTHOR'S NOTE

Some of these essays, together with the appropriate prose on short lines, were written during the ten-year period following on a breakdown in 1945, and others were recorded as epilogues for Tyne Tees Television nine years ago, and so there may be occasions when the substance of my thinking is iterated. The essays recorded as epilogues have been marked with a ↄ.

LET ME MAKE MYSELF PLAIN

I am known as a writer of novels, but my husband, bless him, has always maintained that I am a poet. However, my idea of a true poet is derived from the writings of men such as Donne, Wordsworth, Byron, Shelley, Keats, and in modern times, Betjeman, and each of these is understandable to the ordinary person, except perhaps Donne, who needs some probing. At the same time I also hold that writers such as the often ridiculed Ella Wheeler Wilcox were genuine poets; she, in particular, could transmit homespun philosophy. Like Kipling, she was a poet for the people.

Still, what does this leave me? Not a poet; oh no, because what I put down in this form of writing has neither true rhyme nor rhythm. It is merely, to my mind, Prose On Short Lines.

But over the years I have come to think it rather odd that most of the stuff I write down in this form concerns the spirit. Not the word which is usually associated with organised religion; no, when I talk of spirit I'm thinking simply of that elusive something in each of us, that thing that cries out to be understood, that thing that is a need, a want. All right, call it God if you like, but this word conjures up the old picture that dies hard of heaven and hell, a cushy cloud for goodness or retribution for sin.

This Prose On Short Lines nearly always is the result of my probing, or of the essence of pain, both physical and mental.

9

After leaving the Catholic Church I was adrift and searching madly for a spiritual lifebelt. I tried most denominations, but found them all wanting, and myself still more wanting. This was a very traumatic time for me: I had no longer a prop to lean on, no intermediary to God, I really was in the wilderness.

I have always been looked upon as a strong character, an individualist, and I suppose that, up to a point, this is true; but underneath there was this frightened, lonely, insecure being who during one period ate through my façade and gave me a breakdown; and then I did need help.

Having read almost every book that had been written about people in a similar spiritual situation, I was still no nearer to finding that prop. Then came the day I revolted and actually spoke to God, not through the Virgin Mary or the Holy Family or the Saints, or even Jesus himself. I'd always had to go through the lot to get to Him – but here I was, this day, facing Him and actually swearing at Him: I told Him I was fearing Him no more – I'd been brought up to fear Him – but from now on, I said, I was going it alone. I'd fought before and won, and somehow I'd fight this thing: I'd find peace of mind and spirit without recourse to dogma or doctrine, or I would die in the attempt, and then take the consequences should I find a governing body on the other side.

For a few seconds after this brave show I experienced a feeling of ecstatic freedom. It didn't last.

Many years have gone by since that time and I have sorted the specks of spiritual gold from the dross, and one saying of the man from Galilee has become like a lodestar to me: THE KINGDOM OF GOD IS WITHIN YOU.

The kingdom, in my case, is that inner strength, the strength of spirit that brought me through the years of the breakdown.

I am still having to put up a fight now and then against the residue of those years, and I find it strange that it is during these periods of depression or fear that I'm driven to write my bits of homespun philosophy. Looking back, I can actually check my bad periods through these essays, and so, where I have thought it appropriate, I have woven one or two of them into the mouth of a character in one of my stories. But as for making them into epilogues, it never, never crossed my mind.

However, one day, I was being interviewed for a programme on Tyne Tees Television by two researchers, Miss Heather Ging and Mr Malcolm Gerrie, and after listening to my reading of a piece of my Prose On Short Lines, they surprised me somewhat by asking for more. Then they said, 'We know who would be interested in these.'

'Who?'

'Maxwell Deas, the head of religious broadcasting at Tyne Tees.'

'What for?'

'Epilogues.'

'EPILOGUES? You're kidding! EPILOGUES?'

They weren't, and the outcome was a visit from Maxwell Deas; and my first words to him were:

'NOW LET ME MAKE MYSELF PLAIN, I'm an agnostic.'

But this didn't seem to matter, and from any time after midnight on a number of Saturday nights onwards I tried to do just that, make myself plain.

This resulted in my receiving letters asking for copies of the talks and poems, and not a few inquiries if I were going to publish them.

Again this hadn't entered my mind; but when I began to think about it, I saw there was a snag, a big one in my opinion. When one is putting over something through speech, there is the inflection, the facial expression, and, in my case, the use of the hands to give point and emphasis to what one is saying; but the same topic presented in print takes on a different form; the reader is 'listening to' a disembodied voice coming from the page. Yet, I thought, if the epilogues were to appear in book form I would wish

11

for them to be presented undiluted, and stand or fall in the process.

Since a breakdown has been the main crisis in my life and has left such a residue of mental anguish, on which, curiously, my writing career has been nurtured, I may seem to dwell much on its effects, but I do so with a purpose in the hope that, in making myself plain, perhaps one person, just one, may be helped to rise above the fear of God, or the feeling of inadequacy created by being childless, or the utter misery of a breakdown, or just the daily depression engendered by the struggle to get through this life.

I am including some of my drawings and paintings, too, because, in a way, it was the drawings which were probably instrumental in bursting the boil of the breakdown, whereas the paintings helped to bring colour back into my life from the time of my returning to the North eleven years ago.

From areas of longing
That fill my life with strife
To stretch my intellect
To those of whom I read
And express my doubt
In high-flowing
Screed
That would bewilder
All,
In turn,
As I am
By minds
That burn
To impress,
Thus transgressing
The art to convey,
I pray you,
God of Words,
Keep me simple
For this day.

PHILOSOPHY

If I hadn't been brought up in an atmosphere of want, drink, and ceaseless hard work, threaded with faint veins of love and unexpected and less-understood spurts of joy, I should not now be known as Catherine Cookson the writer, because this environment was the womb in which my imagination was bred.

That I refused to accept this fact until the umbilical cord was severed by a breakdown I now look upon as part of the plan that was designed at my conception when my mother committed the unforgivable sin of giving herself in love to a man without words having first been spoken over them by a parson, a priest, or a registrar.

The kitchen of 10 William Black Street, East Jarrow, in the County of Durham was a world of its own. It was ruled over by my step-grandfather, John McMullen, a drunken, ignorant Irishman, who could neither read nor write; a man who worked hard, said little and was lost on the empty plane of his silence and ignorance but who nevertheless was the only man in my young life, and the one who has left the most lasting impression.

It was this old man who first told me I had two of the main ingredients that go to make a writer, a vivid imagination and, as he said, sprouting from that I was a natural liar.

John McMullen was feared by most people; somehow I was never afraid of him. As he once said to me, he had never wished me to be born, but then he had made the best of a bad job, and we had shaken hands on it.

14

It was evident all my young days that he was the man in my life. This was made clear every night when he came in at tea-time and sat down to a meal of either finny haddie and new bread, or steak and chips, or panhackelty. But always he would start the meal with an egg, and I had to have the top of it; the top meant the egg being cut in half, and he would scoop the contents on to a piece of dripping and bread and hand it to me, and I would stand by his side and eat it.

I often wondered over the years why I couldn't have an egg to myself, but no, as I said, he was the man in my life, he was the man who was bringing me up, feeding me, and this had to be made evident. Of course, no credit was given to my mother who worked sixteen hours a day, often eight hours outside the house and eight hours in, looking after him and my ailing grandmother and a half-brother and numerous lodgers. No credit was ever given to her, she was just Our Kate, and she had sinned grievously; she should thank her stars that she had a roof over her head and she wasn't in the workhouse, and me along of her.

In those days at the beginning of the century there were many such people as Kate and myself but who were less fortunate and who'd had to find refuge in the workhouse, and there the mother was forced to remain until the child was fourteen and could itself go out to work.

Years later when I went to work in South Shields Workhouse I shuddered inwardly as I looked at some of the inmates and thought, There but for the grace of God goes our Kate. And when I had to take mothers to the cottage homes I would repeat the saying as I looked at the children: There, but for the grace of God, goes me.

But all the while I was gaining something, a philosophy you could say. I was learning that philosophy isn't the prerogative of the academic, the intellectual, all those supposedly knowledgeable people who blind you with the science of the mind. Philosophy is, as I saw it then and still do, the essence of the thinking of every ordinary man and woman. It is the sum total of what they have drained out of their living whether through sorrow or joy, satisfaction or frustration.

I have come to my own particular philosophy by being educated in a hard school where lessons of poverty, shame, inferiority, fear and ill-health were hard to learn. But my philosophy evolved, as I see it now, in my fight against these afflictions. I was helped, I suppose, in its fostering by my vivid imagination, my sensitivity and my groping to understand my fellow creatures, those nearest to me.

But, even so, it was slow to evolve and, of course, I wasn't conscious that I was learning the lessons of life when I attacked my afflictions with aggressiveness and ambition. It wasn't really until I learned to apply the salve of compassion to the wounds of my own life that I realized I had garnered one grain of wisdom.

I could wish I had become wise to do so many things much earlier, but then it is in the blissfulness of ignorance that so much is learned and achieved, and this, I suppose, is the basic purpose of life.

Whenever I speak of me granda or Our Kate it recalls the kitchen of 10 William Black Street and I know it was in that room, in which it was difficult to move, that my mind first began to expand; and the atmosphere was revived for me the other night during a power cut.

I'd forgotten the sight of an open fire
And got used to the artificial electric glow;
It took a power cut amidst the snow
To bring back the ecstatic state
Of glowing coals in a grate.

I saw again the kitchen:
The fire bars sizzling red
And, standing on the hob,
The big black pan of stew
In which I slyly dipped me bread;
My nose was filled with perfume
From the oven's heavenly smell,
And in that fleet but everlasting moment
I knew that all was well.

My bare feet on the steel fender
Soaking up the heat,
My Granda playing patience
At which he never failed to cheat,
Kate underneath the gas lamp
Cooking for the morrow,
My heart and mind lost in a book
I'd been fortunate enough to borrow.

The joys of childhood are brief:
Like mist they fade
And are lost in life's rut,
But sometimes, just sometimes,
The gods are kind
And let you glimpse them again,
Through a power cut.

MARRIAGE

We hear of girls of thirteen giving birth to babies. . . . What do I think about it? I think, Poor souls! What they must go through, not only during the agony of birth, but also during the longest nine months they are likely to experience in their lives.

Then there is 'the boy friend'. In my young days the term would have implied that a couple were courting; but now the connotation has been extended, and is so often highlighted in the media as to create the acceptance of infidelity. But marriage is still fashionable. And yes; so it seems is divorce. However, I read that this is slowly taking a back seat in the USA, and since we usually follow their trends, let's hope.

I, myself, look upon marriage as an ocean; it has its stormy parts, but there are lots of lovely islands in it.

I didn't marry until I was thirty-three. I was six years older than him. I was an extrovert, he an introvert. I was taller than him; at least I used to think so in those days, in my high-heeled shoes. Outwardly we were utterly unsuited; everybody said so: it would never last; it was fated from the beginning. So they hoped; and they waited for it to end; a few, I know, prayed for just that. Well, perhaps God used us as an experiment when He threw us into our particular ocean. He's let a few storms hit us; and there have been clashes on board ship, mostly to determine who was captain. In the end we decided it was better to be second mates.

And so we've steered for some of those lovely islands. Sometimes we didn't stay long on them, mind, and the weather blew up here and there; but, when all's said and done, our voyage of marriage has been a good trip.

It has proved one thing, at least to me: if your heart tells you a thing is right, tell your head to mind its own business; your heart, after all, is in most cases the better judge of a mate.

A Mate

A mate is different from a husband;
A mate, when he leaves your side, is still with
    you:
He is the flesh below the hide,
He is ever present in your work-filled mind,
And in the blind depths below;
He is with you when the sun is on your face,
Or life has brought you low;
He is with you when your friends turn false;
He is with you in that exchanged glance
Or in silences that are loud with love;
He is with you in your off days
When the mirror shows the lined pattern of your
    face,
Or when your heart has forgotten to sing.
Your mate is not the dream lover the night brings,
For he vanishes with the light.
No; your mate is that nondescript fellow,
    six-foot-two or five-foot-three,
Who, under life's buffets, never breaks, just bends;
Your mate is the one you can rest assured on
Right to the end.

So

MARRIAGE

Let's drink to us, mate!
Lift up your glass, your cup, your mug, and drink
   to us.
No quips about a dirty week-end,
The excitement of another's wife to take away the
   boredom of life;
No need to gawp at a stripping male
Or make up laughter at a lewd joke;
Let's drink to us ordinary folk, mate, and the
   married state.

Don't be ashamed of being happily wed,
Whether at the registry office or the altar rail;
Don't let the thought of it make you quail;
And don't believe that a change is as good as a
   rest,
Your own bed will prove to be best;
So lift up your glass, your cup, your mug, mate,
And drink to us in the married state.

BILL

It's an awful confession to make but, being without mother, father, sister or brother, there is no one in my life I have missed as I did Bill. When Bill died I knew sorrow deep and terrible; terrible because I was afraid of it, afraid of being the kind of person that could almost go to pieces through the loss of an animal.

But was Bill an animal? Not to me he wasn't; Bill was a special being who loved me. For a period of nine years he altered my life: he caused me more trouble, tears and worry than enough. He was the ugliest bull-terrier that ever lived – so a number of people told me – but to me he was beautiful.

Besides introducing me to trouble, Bill brought me in touch with a number of odd people and some hilarious situations. In the first place it was funny how we came to have Bill. A friend of ours heard we wanted a dog and said, 'Oh, I've got the very thing, it's a bull-terrier and its owner wants to get rid of it. She's gone away for a month and left it with me. I must confess though,' he added, 'it's the runt of the litter.'

Bill was a Staffordshire brindle, and even as a puppy had a chest on him like a heavyweight. From the word go we knew we were made for each other. However, for the first few weeks together life was a mixed blessing. We found from the start that Bill had a weakness for material, any material, and his duty in life, he imagined, was to tear it

21

into shreds. Until we learned some sense the house was full of feathers, flocks and kapok.

But about odd characters. During this initial period a lady came to the door and said she wanted her dog, or . . . ten pounds. Apparently she had never intended to give it away, it had all been a big mistake. But I could have the dog for ten pounds.

At the time we were very hard up and if we'd had ten pounds it wouldn't have gone on a dog, as much as I wanted one. Seeing my distress, she said, 'Well if you want him, you'll buy him.'

When I told her I hadn't ten pounds to spare, uninvited, she walked around the hall and, picking up an antique brass bucket and various other items, she stated, 'I'll take those for him.'

I love my bits and pieces and I was indignant at the whole affair and told her to take the dog and to get out.

From her arms Bill looked at me. He put out one beseeching paw and howled. And I rushed indoors and I howled.

Tom said, 'Well, if you feel like that, give her the bucket and the odd stuff.' I didn't need a second bidding; I dashed out to see Bill at the back window of the car. The woman was driving very slowly, she had weighed me up.

When she stopped the car I grabbed up Bill and said, 'Come and get them.'

She came back smiling, picked up the five pieces of brass, then left, still smiling.

Our friend who had let us have the dog was incensed. He saw his friend, a solicitor, who happened to be the husband of the lady and who, apparently, couldn't believe it.

Result, a private car appeared, and the driver brought out all my bits and pieces of brass and a letter of apology.

The day I took Bill to be inoculated he made a great fuss and the vet said, 'Good lord; what a baby! And he isn't a thoroughbred, you know, he's all odds and ends.'

On our way down the road from the surgery Bill got his

first smell of a butcher's shop. My mind was on the vet's words, when there was a sharp tug and I found myself on the end of the lead doing a flying tour round the butcher's chopping block, and in the process entangling with the butcher, his assistant and three customers. I was shouting I'd be back and pay when, with a piece of meat in his mouth, Bill drew me out of that shop like a cork out of a champagne bottle and along the sea front, to the amazement of the strollers, for you don't usually see a full-grown woman galloping at top speed at the end of a dog lead.

But within the next three months one thing proved to be true: Bill definitely was the runt of the litter for he caught everything, including mange. Bull-terriers are subject to mange, I understand. Bill's hair fell out and his body became covered with sores. Twice daily I had to apply liniment to these sores, and this sent the poor animal almost berserk; but never once did he turn on me.

Now it was my turn to be covered with spots. My face and neck were ablaze with small red pimples which the doctor said was likely caused by scurf from my hair. Scurf from my hair indeed!

When the red rash reached to my toes I went to the doctor again, and he declared himself puzzled. 'Have you been abroad?' he asked.

'Abroad!' I said. 'No; I've been too busy nursing my dog.'

'What's wrong with your dog?'

'Mange,' I said.

'My God! woman,' he said; 'you've got the mange. Trust you to get the mange.'

And I had the mange. One in a million get the mange, and I'm one in a million where disease and infections are concerned.

I arrived home with the remedy, a three-inch paint brush and a huge bottle of white liquid, which under other circumstances and in other places would be called 'sheep-dip'. It was the depth of the winter and snowing and we were on fuel rationing at the time. But the prescription had

23

to be carried out to the letter or else the mange and I would be companions for a long time.

In a room that was barely warm I stripped off my clothes, and my husband performed the operation of painting me from head to foot in the sheep-dip. When the stuff dried I felt I was encased in cement, and for three days, covered only in a loose dressing-gown, I remained in that room. But it did the trick. The stuff also did the trick for Bill.

Until Bill was two years old he was goofy: he was friendly disposed to dogs of all types, and passionately attached to people, especially to toddlers whom he would bump gently with his nose, causing them to sit down abruptly, when he would sit down beside them. I never knew one to cry from this treatment. He was the favourite of postmen, dustmen, in fact of all humanity, until the day he had a disagreement with his pal next door after un-earthing his bone. The labrador just went for him, and to Bill's complete amazement he found himself on his back and in no friendly tussle but being torn literally to shreds. His face bore the scars until the day he died.

It was from this time that Bill's hatred of his own kind became the nightmare of our life. This hatred of his urged him to roam looking for trouble, and he defied every effort of ours to keep him in. The times I have gone round our neighbourhood calling, 'Bill! Bill! where are you? Bill! Bill, darling.' I think I became known as 'the batty woman who owned the bull-terrier'. Whenever I would go up to anyone they would know exactly what I was going to say: 'Have you seen a bull-terrier?' Sometimes I would find him gambolling in a field, nearly always with the same lady. He never quarrelled with her. She lived about two miles away but she had only to send a telepathic message, which he received loud and clear and which he answered as soon as was doggedly possible. He always left a message to say how he had gone: sometimes it would be chewed wire netting, sometimes ripped railings, at others it would be a foot-deep channel.

When it was utterly impossible for him to get out he would call passing dogs to him by making a quite friendly noise, but once they squeezed through the bars of the gate which were too narrow for him to get his chest through, he would immediately set upon them. This cruel procedure upset Tom very much. It always lay with him to get Bill off the dogs, which he had to do by forcing a walking stick between his teeth. I have seen Tom almost on the verge of collapse after getting him free.

The only cure, so we were told and urged to carry out, was to thrash him after a fight. In desperation Tom tried this. He thrashed Bill, he thrashed this big fierce bull-terrier who never once turned on him, but who, the thrashing over, would crawl up to him and lick his hand. It was too much. Our nerves were frayed, something would have to be done. But what?

The decision came one day when Bill hesitated for a fraction of a second before making the choice of attacking an elkhound or going and kissing its young owner. We were on to him before he could move either way; but it decided us, we couldn't risk a child being hurt. We were confident Bill would never hurt a child intentionally but terrible things could happen unintentionally. The final decision lay with me and I made it, but I couldn't stay in and await the vet's coming to fetch him. He was to come at eleven. I returned home at one, expecting to find the yard empty. Certainly there was no bouncing dog coming towards me. Bill always bounded to me and when I bent down to him he nipped at my ears very gently. But Bill was still with us, he was sitting against the wall, his body pressed tight to it, his cheek pressed tight to it, and he didn't look at me.

How does a dog know he is condemned to death? That dog knew.

When the vet eventually came he said it was a shame to put such a fine beast to sleep; he would operate on him. He was rather old for this, being four, but he would try. If it was only aggressiveness that made him go for other dogs it would work but if the instinct was a 'guard instinct' it would have no effect on him. Should I change my mind about having him put to sleep, he said I could phone before midnight when he would let him come round from the anaesthetic, otherwise he would give him another dose.

Bill was led to the gate, from where he turned round and looked at me. I could just see him through my blurred vision, but the expression in his eyes said, 'Why? why are you doing this?' as plainly as if he had shouted it.

The vet couldn't have reached home before I was on that phone. Three days later Bill returned to us, and, further, efficiently demonstrated that his aggressive instinct was – the guard instinct.

As the years went on, life with Bill became one long watch. But could I mind this when of an evening he would pull his great weight on to my lap and put his head under my chin, and in the mornings sneak up to the bedroom – a forbidden place this – climb into bed, turn his back to me and snuggle down and wait for Tom's voice shouting, 'Where is that dog? Where is he?' This was a game during which Bill would not even move a muscle, not even a twitch of his tail, until my husband, throwing the clothes back, would say, 'There you are! you scoundrel,' and Bill would laugh at him. He actually laughed, this dog. His lips would be drawn back from his teeth and the corners of his little eyes would wrinkle and his tongue would come out and he would look from me to Tom, saying plainly, 'Aw, there's nothing like a bit of fun.'

And then one day he died. He was nine years old.

He died in Tom's arms. They were both on the drawing-room rug. I can still see them.

We were devastated, lost. He had been our child, a tearaway, a bad lad but a loving bad lad, and above all he had been MY BILL.

Fourteen Years Later
Simon Followed Bill

Simon, too, died,
And I am hollow:
Pain where my heart was;
Hands blind now
For they feel no thick ruff,
Nor the puff of his breath
As he licked me a kiss.

Thirteen and a half was a good age;
And he died a score
Of times this past year.
So was it fair to wish him life?
Yet he strove to live until the last breath,
When he turned to Tom's
Tear-wet face and gave up the fight.

Oh, Simon, I am hollow
For I loved you.
And told you I did;
And I did not bid for your love
Against Tom,
For you loved him first;
I was content to love you,
And that is love.
And now I am hollow.

HAPPINESS

You cannot sustain joy or wonder; its ethereal quality makes it intangible.

As for happiness as opposed to pleasure: well, you can get pleasure by looking at a picture, and you can repeat that pleasure; but you have to see or feel the object to get the full value of the pleasure; the mere memory of it is always diluted. But happiness is on a different plane: it is a state of mind, the main ingredient of which, I think, stems from kindness; and from this naturally comes giving, warmth, consideration and often religious conviction, in which, although I know it didn't work for me, many people still find utter happiness.

I don't think happiness is anything to do with sex; because happiness has no real heights or depths.

Nor yet do I feel that happiness has anything to do with compassion, although this does hold the ingredients of consideration, but compassion itself, I think, holds the essence of sadness.

Then again, you hear the saying, 'They're never happy unless they're finding fault', but the reaction he or she gets from finding fault couldn't be further removed from happiness; the very action of fault-finding, in my opinion, is to alleviate some lack in oneself.

So many clever brains have tried to explain happiness that I really feel I have a nerve to try; but when all's said and done, it is a personal thing.

Last night I watched my husband baking bread and I felt

28

happy, it even brought a touch of joy to me.

Talking of joy, you know that line, 'There is joy in heaven over one sinner doing penance'? Well, it was so drummed into me at school and Sunday school that every time I went to confession I had a mental picture of THEM ALL UP THERE having a real high time, like people on New Year's Eve, you know, knees-up, the lot, and all because I had promised to be a good girl and control my thoughts about having babies and things.

And then there is wonder. Now wonder is a special kind of happiness, especially the wonder of childhood. My childhood was full of stress, and, as I remember, I was always tired. I look back on the northern days as often dark and the streets dreary. Yet just at times through all this would pierce a light which managed to rend life's dismay asunder. And this is what, I suppose, one could call wonder.

But I ask myself now, why has it gone from life? Was it only lent to children in those days gone by when a penny was a pound and meals meagre? Was it a gift given only to the few to experience?

If I would ask of God a gift I would say: 'Before my time is up, give me back a moment of enchantment; let me just once again know that ecstatic lift, that spiritual glow that wipes away life's tears, life's heartbreaks.' I would pray, 'Not only give me, but give us all, a moment, a tender, out of this world moment in which we might recall and ponder that grace you gave to the child, called wonder.'

Wonderment

A feeling engendered by photographs
and description in *The Arizona Magazine*
published in the USA

I have seen things only God has seen;
I know things only God knows;
I can see the wind and from where it blows;
I feel the power that turns water into snow;
I have sat where the volcano is born;
I have spewed lava and watched the earth
* burn;*
I have made stars out of bangs of heat;
I have flown into infinity and sat at God's
* feet;*
I have grasped the earth in my hand and
* walked with God's Son;*
All this I have done
Looking down on the wonder of the Grand
* Canyon.*

TIME AND THE CHILD

I can smell memories of my childhood. The smell of real manure from a farmyard, as distinct from that of chemicals, recalls the scene of a farmyard outside Shields. I was on high ground. There were rocks and the sea to the left of me, and there away in the distance was a field of corn, red corn.

On closer investigation I found that the edge of the field was rimmed with fragile flower-heads, hundreds and hundreds of them. Kate later told me that they were poppies. I thought the name didn't suit them somehow, they should have been called flamers; and there was no incongruity in the fact that this is what me granda called the people next door.

Perhaps it's old age creeping on or galloping on but I find my mind going back to these days, to episodes in my childhood, more and more.

Here I am, eighty-one, and I know that inside I am still very much the child, the child that was Katie McMullen of East Jarrow; only the façade is the woman and it hasn't the power to control the child. Somehow I can't ignore the power of the child I once was and still am: I am still hurt as she was hurt; I still laugh as she laughed; I still have the secret insight that she had, the insight that recognised sorrow and loneliness in others, the insight that was in me before I suckled milk, for, as our Kate said, if I in her womb had been aware of what she was suffering during those nine months she carried me, then I should surely have been born mental.

Well, I must have been aware of her pain for I nearly went mental, didn't I?

I find that time is galloping away now; it isn't dawn before it's dusk. The hours leap into days and the days disappear into weeks, and I can't remember what I did in them. The pity of it is, my mind at this stage is clearer than at any period in my life, and I long for time, long time, the time of childhood, in which to expand and grow again.

You know, we are what our early environment makes us. I believe that is true. All through our life those early years colour our thinking. No matter how thick the veneer, that environment has a way of kicking itself through the skin. When the race is almost run and the two ends of the circle are meeting you see the child coming towards you, and you go back into his time more and more. You can recognise his thinking more so than when at twelve, thirteen or fourteen you left him behind. The knowledge of his magic is fresh before your eyes, for in his time of being there was no growing, there was no age. You knew people did what they called dying and although they were put into the earth they had gone into the sky; but you were here, there'd be new bread for tea; it was Saturday the morrow and there was no school; Sunday, you'd have to go to Mass; on Monday . . . When was Monday? There was no such thing as Monday, not on a Friday night. Monday wouldn't appear until late on Sunday night when you were dropping off to sleep. And Sunday was a long, long way off. It came after Saturday. But tonight was Friday and tomorrow you would go to the penny matinee at The Crown. What greater joy could anyone ask for?

In that time I can smell baking day in the kitchen. I can see the kitchen as if it were set out before me. There's me sitting on the fender, Kate bustling all around me.

'Move your backside out of that,' she says.

I shuffle along the fender away from the blackleaded oven door, quickly past the fierce blazing fire built up in a

*'Paintings helped to bring colour
back into my life.'*

'My land of deep lakes
With mountain shadows...'

'Tom sat for me and for the first
time in my life I did a portrait,
and I got an amazing likeness.'

*'Poppies were growing
amid the mass of weeds.'*

slant, you know, to keep the heat against the oven, and when I reach the far end of the long fender I say, 'A . . . w!' for the steel is always cold between the end of me knickers and the top of me stockings.

I watch her lift the sneck of the oven door and pull out the oven shelf on which there are four loaf tins; she plonks the shelf on to the fender, dextrously upturns the loaf tins that are as black as the oven itself, gives three taps with her knuckles on the bottom of each tin, nods towards the oven as if acknowledging her debt to it, then looks at me and says, 'Have you got your yule-doo ready? Come on, look slippy if you want to put it in; I haven't got all day.'

I can see myself coming out of my dreaming, jump to the table, pick up the much-fingered piece of dough I've shaped into a man – perhaps this time he has currants for his eyes, mouth and nose, and a row for his coat, or perhaps this time funds were too low for currants and his face is featureless and his suit without buttons. I can see my laying him tenderly on the hot plate. I want to straighten him out, but Kate's voice will have none of it.

'Don't make a meal of it, not yet anyway. Out of me road!'

The oven door bangs on me yule-doo, Kate straightens her back, dusts the palms of her hands loudly against each other, blows a strand of hair from her sweating brow by thrusting out her lower jaw and puffing upwards; then she looks down on me and says gently, I can hear her saying it gently, 'Well, that's done. We'll have a sup tea, eh hinny?'

'Oh aye, Kate. Aye, yes.'

The smell of new bread slides me back into eternity, the eternity that was childhood; the eternity of pain and fear and that sick feeling in my chest caused by fear. The fear that me granda would make a big hole in his pay by dropping into the North-Eastern pub before coming home.

The fear that he might have had a very good week and so

they'd all have a drop too much, and there'd be divils fagarties later on.

The fear there'd be no money on Monday for the rent; and I'd be kept off school to go to Bob's – Bob's was the pawnshop.

The fear that I'd have to miss Mass on Sunday 'cos me boots weren't decent.

The fear of facing the headmistress on the Monday and admit I hadn't been to Mass. Oh, that fear outdid the one on purgatory, hell and damnation.

But, as I said, there were moments of wonder when all these fears were forgotten in that everlasting time by memories of flamers in a field, and the smell of new bread in that kitchen that served so many purposes, and the memory of which will stay with me till I die.

Oh, for the eternity of childhood time
When the morning was New Year's Day
And dinner-time was high summer
And evening was autumn
Falling into December and bed.

Such was a day.

As for a year;
What was a year?
What measure to give to endlessness
Waiting for the Christmas stocking hanging
    on the rod?
Who made the time of childhood?
Did God?

And did He make the silver light
That heralds love's first flight
Into the breast
And causes vows of eternalness
To fall like jewels from the lips?

And did He bring eyes to buttons on breasts
To note their rising to something strange
Not fully understood,
Like motherhood?

Then if He did,
Let me pray
I reach my second childhood
Some day.

CHRISTMAS

Christmas Day, 1974

We have taken the day off. We have been going at it hell for leather for weeks now, from early morning till late at night, seven days a week. The mail has just poured in. But how kind people are: I've had presents from every corner of the world, ranging from hand-knitted dishcloths and lavatory roll covers to a set of silver eggcups, not forgetting the Christmas stocking sent me by a lady. Having read in my autobiography how disappointed I was the Christmas I got nothing but vegetables in the sailor's bag, this kind person thought up an idea of a Christmas stocking, and what a Christmas stocking. It had in it about seventeen different kinds of sweets, besides numerous presents. How can one not be humbled by such kindness?

It is 8 a.m. I feel very happy, contented and at peace.

I pray God it may last for a while.

I thank you God
For everything I have this day.
Put aside the Christmas fantasy:
The crib,
The wise men,
The lay;
Put aside goodwill to men
Which rarely holds after Christmas Day;
Put aside the cross,

The chanting,
The Mass;
Put aside the denominations,
The crank sects,
And religious castes;
And what have you?
Still that image called God, come what may,
And whom I thank
For everything I have
This Christmas Day.

Christmas Presents

What do I want for Christmas?

Food,
A little wine,
An easy chair.
Presents? A few –
– And you.

And what will I give you for Christmas?

Love and tenderness,
Dreamless sleep,
Thoughts of your garden in spring
The budding trees –
– And me.

And what do I want for the New Year?

An easy mind,
Hope anew,
A kind heart,
Compassion –
– And you.

And what do I want for you in the New Year?

Peace of mind,
The joy of living and seeing,
The medicine of laughter,
The key to lock out fear,
And to walk, my dear,
Through the days of life –
– With me.

Tom won't let me laugh overmuch and cry not at all, for both emotions cause me to bleed, but today I laughed until my sides ached and with no ill effect. It was a wonderful feeling.

Boxing Day, 1974

Come laughter,
Well up, widen my lips,
Stretch my cheeks,
Bring tears to my eyes
And make me weep with mirth.
Come from your secret place
Where you are conceived by
Differing wits;
Come, give birth to cheer
And send to the winds
Boredom, depression and fear.

Come laughter, come
Stay with me while I breathe,
And when I can use you
No more,
Not even bring to my lips
Your shadow of a smile,
Still linger in my memory
To lighten my passage
From shore to shore.

PRIESTS

When I was fifteen and in service, just marking time before I became a great novelist, or a great painter, or found my father who would whip me off into his mansion, educate me and make me into a lady, or arrange for me to marry a rich gentleman who would realise that I was different from anyone else he had ever met – and perhaps he wouldn't have been far wrong then because I must have been barmy, the ideas I had. Anyway, it was at some point in the marking-time period that I first decided I might as well be a nurse, and so I went to Father Bradley because, in those days, in my environment, it was the priest who recommended you for a job in the workhouse. Father Bradley was on the Board of Guardians, and he knew everyone who sat under his pulpit on Sunday, and as he had seen me gazing at him for years and had surely noticed my wide-stretched eyes and intent interest – not knowing it was the only way I could stop myself falling asleep – he would surely give me a good reference.

The interview was very short.

'Father,' I said, 'I want to get into Harton Workhouse an' be a norse.'

He looked down his long snooty nose at me for some seconds before he said, 'You cannot be a nurse. For one reason, you're not old enough; and what's more, you haven't had the required education.'

Eeh! the things I said about that priest: I had to go to confession, but not to him of course.

The second interview I had with him was briefer still.

Since I was fifteen I'd kept company with a number of lads from the Catholic Boys' Club. We met most Saturday nights in the schoolroom for a dance, the music provided by the piano and anybody who would knock a tune out of it. Those were happy nights. All my first beaux were pit lads; and then I met THE GENTLEMAN.

I don't know how many times the gentleman dropped me and picked me up again during the two years we were going together, but it was sometime during the early period of our acquaintance that, heartbroken, I decided to become a nun. Well, it wasn't surprising, for every Catholic girl at one time or another wanted to become a nun.

Again I went to the priests' house. If I remember rightly the housekeeper's name was Miss Nelson. She let me in as if I were a Protestant. Her eyes said, you're the one who goes with all the lads, you're fast. Well, I suppose I was, you see, because by this time I'd been out with three pit lads and was now 'going with' an insurance agent. Yet on my way to the Presbytery a woman had stopped and told me how good I was. So high was her praise of my virtues that I took it as a sign. I remember she wanted me to persuade her niece, who was a fellow officer in the workhouse, to stop keeping company with a married man. I could do it, she said; her niece would take notice of me because I was such a good lass. I wish I had got her to put that in writing.

Anyway, there I was confronted by Father Bradley.

'Yes?' He peered at me as if he had never seen me in his life before.

'Please, Father,' I said . . . 'Well,' I said, 'I've been thinking,' I said. 'Well, you see, Father, it's like this. Mind you, Father, it isn't the day or yesterday I've had this in me mind, but . . . well, something happened and so I thought that . . . well . . . I thought that . . . I want to be a nun, Father.'

I remember how he continued to peer at me. He peered me up and down and through me. I knew then it was right what me granda said about him thinking himself first cousin to God! Only he didn't say it exactly like that, there was much more to it. Anyway, I knew Father Bradley had always been able to see into my mind and all that went on there. He knew what I thought about at night before I went to sleep – and that after having said my prayers on my knees on the cold lino. But as I told Father O'Keefe every week, there were some things you couldn't stop yourself thinking. Here, though, was the first cousin to God reading my mind again, and it was anything but good reading.

I can see him now walking to the door and opening it and saying grimly, 'Go! . . . And think some more.' I went out with my head almost between my knees . . .

A few nights later, when Kate and I were standing on the step having a chat, as we always did before I returned to the workhouse, I said to her on a painful laugh, 'I think I'll go and be a nun.' She didn't know anything about my having been to Father Bradley.

'Aw, don't lass,' she said in mock seriousness; 'they've enough troubles in the convent and they haven't done you any harm.' And we leant against each other and laughed.

Such little memories as these obliterate the pain of a lifetime.

St Alban's Abbey

ANOTHER TANGENT

The drawing of St Alban's Abbey, I recall now, was not the first drawing I ever did although it is marked as such. It was, in fact, the drawing of a pelvis I attempted when working as an assistant manageress in the laundry of the workhouse in South Shields.

Some long time before, having decided that I was worth something better than my present job, I again thought I would go in for nursing. I was twenty, but the stumbling block of education still remained, so I decided to do something about it, at least with regard to the training to be a nurse. I bought what was called *The Naval Book*. This had been prepared for the training of young men in the Navy to become sick-bay attendants, and had everything in it except a maternity section. However, through its pages I became acquainted with physiology and anatomy. And I recall, on my Sundays off when I would be at home, I would sit at that little table under the window and copy the bones of the body. I remember becoming fascinated with the pelvis and the shadows therein.

I did not go into nursing. I applied to a Newcastle hospital – it was no use trying for the hospital within the workhouse for, there, a failed nurse could be downgraded from the hospital to the house side, but never the reverse could happen. As for my application to Newcastle, I was told it was at the end of a very long list. In any case, I later learned the lack of a birth certificate would have meant rejection.

So, to my second attempt at drawing.

It should happen that I was married on June 1 1940. The following month my husband, the school, and I were evacuated to St Albans.

In our little flat in Victoria Street I spent the time, up to the 7th December that year when my premature baby of six months was born dead, reading and writing. Part of my writing was the composing of a book of rhymes for five-year-olds, supposedly written by my son David. I knew he was going to be a boy and had already given him a name. They were simple rhymes, some telling a story, and some short, such as:

> He said the clock wanted taking to bits
> And when I did it he nearly had fits.
> Fancy making such an e . . . nor . . . mous
>   scene!
> Why do people never say what they mean?

Following the loss of my baby I continued with the book, and decided it would be much improved if the rhymes were illustrated.

Further up the street was the Art School. I went there and asked if one of the students would do the illustrations. The teacher said the students were all young and that she didn't think they were up to it. Why didn't I come and take lessons myself? She was a very nice lady.

So I went. A thirty-four-year-old seemingly 'old girl' sat amongst the youngsters, much to their amusement, and discovered that it was impossible for her to draw children; in fact, to draw anything. So, after my third appearance, I left.

Some time later, I was taking a walk across the Abbey green when I suddenly stopped and looked up at that pile of stone, and from out of nowhere a voice said, You could draw that. And I answered, Yes; yes, I could draw that.

I scurried back to Victoria Street and into the little stationery shop next to the Art School, and to a surprised lady behind the counter I said, 'I want to draw stone. Can you advise me on pencils?'

This very kind and helpful lady said, 'Well, my dear, now what you'll need are two pencils, one academy chalk and the other a carbon crayon.' They sounded like words of a foreign language. She then added, 'But you might find those pencils too soft to begin with, they take some getting used to. Take a nice HB to start with. And of course, you'll need a pad . . . Now there! Draw your stone.'

I went straight back to the Abbey green, sat down and drew the picture of St Albans (p. 41). She was right; I had to use the HB, but the result fired me with enthusiasm. I framed my picture with passe-partout, I felt so proud of it.

So proud that when invited to a certain master's house to tea I took it along to show him and his wife. I can see him now. He took it in his hands, looked at it hard, then said, 'Did you have to have it framed?' After that I tied my enthusiasm to a great rock and threw it in the river.

And it wasn't until the end of 1942, after losing a second baby and following Tom half-way round the country, that I found myself in Hereford and once again looking at a pile of stone, and the urge returned, and, this time using the academy chalk and carbon crayon, I attacked this massive edifice of stone, the cathedral.

Hereford Cathedral

The South Transept

LOVE

Love means different things to different people. The very young can visualise no pain in love; the teenager sees the death of love as the death of life; the young married woman is forced to realise it has many faces and that some of them are not at all romantic; the mother faces up to the fact that love has to be shared, and often her partner, being unable to accept this, goes searching for the elusive elsewhere; the divorced woman experiences exclusive pangs of love known only to the rejected; the widow is often filled with hitherto unknown love for the departed; the ageing put out hands to clutch love.

To most people love conjures up the vision of happiness, but to me, love holds all the pains of life, with happiness merely the thread that links them together.

Love

Love to me is the terror of being parted;
The suffering of my loved one's pain.
Love to me is the anguish of death,
Not of being deprived of life
But of never seeing him again.

Love to me is boosting his ego,
Making him bigger than all men I know;
Of showing my gratitude,
Not meagrely, not slow
But with touch
And voicing words
That strike the answering chords of love
And bring to his eyes that tender glow.

Love to me is fear of the moments
That I might waste in discord, or bitterness;
The fear that I might survive to mourn their
   loss
And remember that those moments stretched to
   an hour
And the hour to a day,
And that I had thrown some part of my
   fleeting life away.

My love is a rare thing,
But do not envy it to me,
For who would want such agony.

LOVE

As I said, I don't fear Death, but I do fear being left without Tom for he has been my stay, my right hand, and comfort for forty-seven years. We often discuss our parting, and he fears it more than I, if that is possible. I say to him: 'When I go, take all the money and buy yourself a yacht and sail the seas,' for this has been his lifetime's desire, but he just looks at me as if to say, 'Don't be silly.'

What shall I do when he goes?

Only God knows.

> *Don't leave me, beloved, on this plane*
> *Without your hand to grasp in the night*
> *And your voice to wake me from sleep*
> *And your love to wrap my day in kindness,*
> *Fold on fold,*
> *And tell me that I'm young,*
> *And that age*
> *Could never make me old.*

> *Don't leave me, beloved, to wither*
> *Without your touch.*
> *Take me when you go;*
> *Take me with you over the brink*
> *That separates death from life.*
> *Don't leave me in the dark existence of my*
>   *being*
> *For I am but a reflection of despair*
> *When you are not there.*

> *Don't leave me, beloved, without an aim,*
> *Don't take the spark that ignites,*
> *Don't leave me desolate of your light,*
> *For how could I see through the days ahead;*
> *Without your presence near me*
> *I've gone before you,*
> *I'm already dead.*

> *Who would of their free will,*
> *Choose such love?*

LOVE

I have relations, I have friends, I have thousands of friendly acquaintances; there are people that I like and people that I dislike: but standing apart there is only him.

> *Morning and high noon and evening*
> *Don't make a day;*
> *Or night and dawn;*
> *Or the elements that fill the hours*
> *With sunshine, wind or rain;*
> *Or yet again great events,*
> *Disasters, wars or hurricanes;*
> *Or other folks' loves;*
> *Or hate or fear;*
> *But the seconds with you,*
> *And you only, dear.*

Tom has suffered from migraine for thirty-nine years. He has a cluster of them which can span a period of three to four days. It is impossible for him to lie down during these attacks and so he sits in a chair in a darkened room downstairs. At these times I find it impossible to sleep and keep getting up to see how he is, and he keeps sending me back to bed. This can go on and on, night after night, until we are both worn out.

Looking back over the years and the countless bouts he's suffered I don't know how we've accomplished the work we have.

The Bed

This bed is a desert, hot-ridged and hard;
This bed is a sea devoid of fish,
A sky without stars,
A planet cold and stark;
This bed is the lark without its song,
A locust-eaten farm,
A dead tree;
This bed is me
Without you.

Bring water to the desert,
Bring fish to the sea,
Bring stars to the sky,
Life to the planet,
Song to the bird,
Growth to the farm,
Life to the tree,
Come to bed and lie with me.

Our Thirty-Eighth Wedding Anniversary

This is a day filled with time;
Not ordinary minutes,
Clock ticking, spaced,
But thirty-eight years of time
Packed with struggle, love,
And tragedy faced,
Back to back
Barricading each other
Against the bombardment
Of life;
Our defences, arrow-pierced
Not infrequently with joy,
And shared thought that makes
Us one in all but body;
This day of thirty-eight years
Not free from strife,
But no one of which
I would bury;
This is a day filled
With all time
And endless life.

The Effect of Beauty

Beauty never brings me joy without pain,
So why do I long to be stabbed again?
The falling snow, illuminated rose
From the sinking orb of the winter sun,
Floats down in spell-binding charm to those
Who on their past turn no blind eye and run
But stay their gaze,
Slaves, to be entranced,
While I, half sage, half child,
Beg my spirit be enhanced,
Uplifted, gay, made young and credulous
   again.
Instead, my heart opens to an agony:
Why do I, a coward in the flesh,
Seek pain?

THE SLUMP

The Slump, 1930

From Birtley to Shields,
Walking singly,
In two's,
Or grouped,
Dark clothed,
Capped;
This Sunday morning
Standing in sockets
Of doors,
With hands in pockets . . .
Why do the men
Walk so?
Stiff from shoulder to hip,
No easy stride . . .
When forearm is locked
To the side.

Was it as bairns,
Their noses running cold,
Blue, numb,
Their eyes gummed with rime,
Feet like long dead flesh,
That caused their hands
To seek burial?

All along the way
On this summer's day
Like manacled slaves they go,
Hands in pockets

53

THE SLUMP

Faces showing no glow,
The men of the North.

Jarrow, 1964

I view you not, Jarrow, through
the misty, nostalgic glow of love;
around whose skirts I trailed my youth
and rattled into the grey drab bosom
of your streets on the tram;
nor does the memory
of flamed skies,
last breath of dying slag,
touch my heart,
except to know
its glow
told me that men still sweated
to earn dignity, and bread,

And dreamed not yet
of hands turned white,
like lilies,
on the graves of their idleness,
nor saw themselves
shadows of lost youth
clumping through bone-chilling dawns
from Simonside tip,
spent cinders spilling
from their barrows,
on their way back
to Jarrow, dead Jarrow.

Yet, tho' I view you not
through love,
you draw me, in the wide-eyed night,
up the river that washes your feet,
the river on which I played

fifty years ago,
but as I walk
your new broad shining streets,
I see them with no joy,
only as a façade
covering the men and women
of my time;
for they are in my marrow;
they, who the new generation
would forget,
they are my Jarrow.

All right, you've had your say,
you've relived your memories.
Then why not call it a day
and face the fact
your Jarrow is no more;
no longer a blot on the land
begging pity, as of yore,
but part of the North East,
this esoteric ground
on which is found,
as in no other,
a bond of bigot,
hero and sound head;

And from the steel heart
of its past
which pumped out ships,
and from its bowels
evacuated
black diamonds to burn,
there had been born
a new stock,
not less valiant
for ships are still
the heart of this part
and coal the guts.
Now . . . But me no buts.

Nineteen Eighty

I am a heretic;
I will not believe
In resurrection.
The youth of the Tyne
Must not die again
At corner ends,
Or smoke down their tabs
To lips that burn,
Or yearn for labour
For their hands,
Or march in bands
To claim the right to eat.
They must not die
When a yard shuts.
I say again, But me no buts.

Some people have difficulty in recalling scenes from child-hood. That has never been the case with me, for I'm cursed, or blessed, whichever way you look at it, with being able not only to recapture scenes from my earliest times, but also to recall the atmosphere and the very odour of them. Such a memory is of the chimney breast. It was at the end of the street and had been intended to be the focal point of another kitchen of a house that had not been built, and we children played in it. It is this scene which links up many years later with the natural outcome of a marriage.

Learning

We played Ma's and Da's
Those years ago,
Ma's apron and skirt,
Da's shirt and old bowler,
Round the top corner
In the chimney breast;
We played at houses
In which the test was birth.
Our Jimmy,
Three years old,
Played the bairn
New-delivered into the house
In the chimney breast,
And he yelled,
Not like any new flesh
Feeling air upon its skin,
But him, he yelled for taffy,
Which was his pay
For playing the bairn
That day.

Now today,
He stands shivering
Outside the bedroom
From where he hopes
His first-born
Will yell.
No taffy the day,
No pay.
Just sweating hell,

And dim surprise
That from the dole queue,
The Gap,
The Guardians' food ticket,
The corner end,
The tip,
The Man
Somewhere in him not quite spent
Had the virility
To earn the two bob
ALLOWED FOR a bairn
By the government.

Nineteen Eighty-Six

The river is now quiet:
Few bows cleave its waters,
And no clashing clarion clammer of hammer on rivets
Draws you to a yard,
There to see the pregnant belly of a boat
Rising from the stocks.
This time we will not have been saved
As in Thirty-Nine by training men to die
While heaping foreign dead on a strange shore,
For then, all politicians knew
That the best cure for a slump
Was a war,
Whereas this time our dead
Will have died where they stood, sat or lay.
The atmosphere will have a field day.
So can you blame youth for saying, Why worry?
Let's make hay,
Sufficient unto the day.

Nostalgia

Oh would the North were as it was
When I was little Katie,
When ships were born from Palmer's womb
And slag-lit scarlet and black night sky
And rivets flew like sparks from stars
And men were proud to work and sweat.

And yet?
This is just reminiscing talk.
No; I would not have the North
As it was
When I was little Katie,
For then no workman owned a car
Or took a holiday across the sea
Nor dare he stand and say to them
'Lad, I'm as good as thee.'

Oh little Katie of long ago,
Of long, long ago.

MY LAND

When I left the North in 1929 I knew little of the area beyond the confines of South Shields and Jarrow. I had been half a dozen times to Newcastle, once to Durham, once to Gilsland, a few times to Birtley. Even in South Shields and Jarrow I knew only main streets. I existed mostly in the circle of Tyne Dock and East Jarrow.

After 1960 I began to make return trips to the North-east and forays into Northumberland and Durham, and often into Cumbria, in search of new areas in which to set my stories.

This is how I view it now.

My land of deep lakes
With mountain shadows
Like ancient cities
Buried and at rest in their depths;
My land of hidden valleys
Dotted with homesteads,
Solitary, aloof;
My land of barren fells,
Scree slopes gripped by hooves of sheep
And rams protective of their own;
My land of skies stretching to infinity,
Blue high sheets of sheer clear light;
My land of mists,
Grey, wet, body soaking mists
That shroud you to a trembling halt;
My land of tones
Fan-lit and sombre,
Heather purples and autumn golds;
Winter white,
Black frost laden nights
Driving hard to spring
And new born grass
And released water
Rushing from its prison of ice.
Oh, my land of sturdy men,
Short, stumpy in part,
And women warm of heart
And worth
And laughing lips,
My land of the North.

MY PRIVATE WAR

Hereford is a nice town, set amidst beautiful countryside, but I cannot think of it, even now after the passage of forty-two years, without a shudder, for it was there the bubble burst.

But give it its due, it was also there that I really learned to draw, that I became a commercial artist and knew I could have been a real artist had I started early enough and had been given tuition.

The war was on and Christmas cards were very hard to get. I had drawn the cathedral, sitting outside of it when able and with the help of a snap when not. The finished article looked nice.

I went into a stationers' and printers' shop and enquired if my drawing could be made into a Christmas card. Yes, I was told. What did Mr Milligan think about it? Who was Mr Milligan? The head of the Art School. Didn't I go to the Art School? No; I'd never been to an Art School. Well, I'd had three lessons but otherwise . . . well, I just drew. I remember the man looked at me for quite a while and said, 'Look; if you've done this without any training, take my advice and go and see Mr Milligan. And yes, I can make this into a Christmas card. How many would you want?' He then added, 'They would sell well in the town, you know. Christmas cards are difficult to get. And it is the local cathedral.'

I don't know how many I had printed but I do know I went round Woolworths and several of the shops, showing them samples. And I cannot remember how many they bought, but I do remember that, after paying for the printing, the paper et cetera, I made a halfpenny on every card that was sold.

I went to see Mr Milligan. He too looked at my drawing a long time. 'Have you done any more like this?' And I said, 'Yes, one or two.'

'Let me see them,' he said.

So I took my other drawings. These, too, he studied for a long time; then he said, 'If you've done these without a lesson, you must come here and then go on to the Slade.'

WHAT WAS THE SLADE?

Within a year I had drawn a number of other cathedrals and he asked if I would have them hung in an exhibition in the town. Great heavens! It was unbelievable. Three of my pencil drawings were hung. The greatest honour to me though was their being placed next to Dame Laura Knight's 'Swans'. Anyway, they got a mention in the paper.

Fame. Fame.

But before this happened, and just before Christmas, the front page of one of the magazines showed choirboys going through an arch towards an altar, the whole scene being lit by candles. I copied it. But what made me send it to J. Arthur Dixon of the Shanklin Press, the Isle of Wight, I'll never know.

It wasn't sent back; instead I was sent five pounds and asked if I had any more such pictures. Like lightning I sent the five pounds back and said, Oh, that wasn't my original work, it was a copy from a magazine. They then asked if I would do other copies for them.

Would I do other copies for them! I was away. I was an artist. At least, I was until they sent me the book from which they wished me to make copies.

Arthur Mee, and his *King's England* county books. In them, places were illustrated by photographs as small as an inch and a half by an inch, a number of them placed within the bounds of a circle.

My memory of the past is unimpaired right up to my time in Hereford, but from then on the electric treatment during the breakdown left blank patches. What I do remember, however, is that J. Arthur Dixon asked me to bring up one of those tiny pictures to eleven by nine inches. The task was impossible. 'I can't do it.' But Tom stepped in. 'Square it,' he said.

'Square it? How do you square it?'

He showed me. So, after he left at 6.30 in the morning for the seven-mile bicycle ride to Madley until he returned

Dutch Interior after Pieter de Hooch

*'The field was rimmed with fragile
flower-heads'*

'My first attempt had no softness in it.'

'The moon buried itself deep in the water.'

'Never a week passed in the early days
that I did not walk along that seafront.'

at six in the evening, I sat most of the day copying, in minute detail through a magnifying glass, and bringing that inch-and-a-half picture up to the required size. Day after day, day after day, for which work I received five pounds, and conjunctivitis in the eyes.

One thing I learned from this work: I knew nothing about perspective. Well, I would just have to learn, wouldn't I? In this I was helped by studying the books of Vicat Cole on perspective. I didn't know then that he had been the Head of the Art School in Hastings. Today I still refer to his books.

It was after reading him that I looked at art with a different eye; and I was amazed at the lack of perspective in many good pictures. I practised perspective further through copying Dutch Interiors, such as those of Pieter de Hooch.

The parquet floors were a marvellous exercise. I recall showing one to the printer in Hereford and he said, 'You've got the art of texture.'

What was texture? 'Well, at least with regards to drawing.'

It appeared that I could make stone, cloth, or wood et cetera appear as such, all with the help of those two pencils, academy chalk and carbon crayon. I've never used any other since.

It was after this I drew the cathedrals that were hung in the exhibition.

The printer helped me in another way. He introduced me to an old artist called Van der Meersh who was then filling in temporarily as a maths master at the Cathedral School, Hereford. He lived with his wife in a large garret in the old part of the town. On the printer's advice I went to him and asked if he would teach me to paint. His reply was: 'Either you can paint or you can't. You may come and watch me.' So on a Saturday afternoon, his only spare time, I went up into that garret, the walls of which were covered and re-covered with his paintings, all of the sea. I said I wanted to paint my husband. He laughed. 'Do a drawing of him,' he said, 'and bring it back.' And strangely, I did just that.

Tom sat for me and for the first time in my life I did a portrait, and I got an amazing likeness. Yet, I had never been able to draw a child. I am still not able to draw a child. . . . Is it a subconscious block? I don't know. I only know that children are very difficult to capture.

Kilpeck Church Door

Tom

I took my drawing and some oil paints to Mr Van der Meersh and he showed me what to do. It took a number of Saturday afternoons to complete that picture; but it is hanging here in the bedroom right opposite to me and, although I say it myself, it is the spit of Tom; as is the large pencil drawing on the other wall. I did that when he was in his RAF uniform.

Mr Smith, my landlady's father, was an old man, retired from the railway many years before. Like me, he was in the house most of the day. I got him to sit for me. The reproduction of that drawing is in my autobiography. I was very proud of that drawing because I had captured the old man's kindly character.

My painting lessons stopped when old Mr Van der Meersh died. Oh, I was sad. I bought his easel, his paints, and his brushes. I work on his easel to this day; his large brushes are still in the jar, some as hard as bricks now, but I keep them there. I don't know what became of his wife because at that time I myself was going through another of life's tests, losing my third baby, and all the trouble of my past was piling on me, and the breakdown was getting ready to burst.

LIFE

I remember waking one morning some years ago. My nose was cold and I sniffed, then peered towards the window. It was half covered with frost. I got up and looked out and the world appeared beautiful. Yet I couldn't fully appreciate it for I was in one of those questioning periods that brought forth the following:

> The morning is bright
> Frost glinting on glass,
> Trees silent of rustle,
> And stiff the grass.
>
> But come one morning,
> Bright with glints on glass,
> Trees silent of rustle,
> And stiff the grass,
> That I shall not see.
>
> Shall I remember the glory of it?
> This I cannot tell, but vow,
> If one wish were mine
> Granted when I pass,
> There will go with me
> A morning as now,
> Frost glinting on glass,
> Trees silent of rustle,
> And stiff the grass.

After writing that I knew I was in for one of those days when a deep blue haze would be pervading everything. I didn't feel inclined to work. That irritating question, Why bother? What was it all for? was nagging at me again. Then out of the blue, as usual, the voice came at me, the voice that swears at me from the mirror, the voice that, in a way belongs to Kate, and she was saying, 'By God! lass, look about you and count your blessings. You'll get something to grumble about afore you're finished. By stars! you will. You can see, hear, walk, and talk, can't you? Well, just think of all those who'd be glad to change places with you at this minute.'

Yes, when I came to think about it, yes, indeed, there would be a number of folks glad to change places with me at this minute.

Yesterday was gone beyond recall and all in it; tomorrow, I might never see it; but I had today. What was I going to do with it? Look in the glass and mourn my wrinkles? bemoan the fate that one cannot take one's talents with one? sit and probe for the answer to why, thirty years after, I should be still dogged by flashes of the breakdown? or was I going to bestir myself, get up and finish that story? go out in the garden and get those billions of leaves swept up? saw wood for the fire? start on cleaning the three-hundred-foot drain on our unadopted road?

I couldn't at that moment make up my mind, but one thing got through to me, the dead would love this day.

The Plan

One part of me
Looks at life
Through a harmonious
Magnifying glass;

The other,
A being who digs
A lone furrow,
Trying to unearth
Answers to questions
Born of fear
As to why I am here,
And for such a short spell.
But further still,
Why be given a mind
That can realize
The futility of this life's span.

There is a streak of cruelty in the plan.

Today

It doesn't matter any more
That age now patterns my face;
It doesn't matter any more
If after death my soul will not
Awake in some celestial place,
Or if I leave no seed of mine
To transmit my beloved ego
And feed on my talents maybe,
Or that my books be remembered
For their titles and not me;
Or that my house and all be sold,
Or that my relatives will say, Not a penny!
I never thought to see the day;
Or that I be buried in clay,
Or burned to dust like sun-dried hay;
But it matters that I cherish
Now this day as all there is.

Silence

I listen to the silence,
For then memories have their sway:
Memories buried in the past,
Too weak to penetrate the day.
But in the silence
I hear them sharp and clear:
Memories of strife,
Struggle and fear,
Creating grief
Without relief.
Yet, in the silence
They are softened,
Muted with age,
And the silence tells me
Each memory was a page
Printed for my life,
A page I had to read,
Then act, to complete the play
That has brought me
To the chapter
In which I comprehend
That in silence was the beginning,
And in silence is the end.

DOCTORS

There was a wartime doctor who attended me in 1940 in St Albans. He had been dug out of cold storage because of the shortage of his fellows: he was a very old man, a retired naval doctor who, I am sure, had not handled a woman since his intern days, except maybe for pleasure. I had him to attend me because I wanted it confirmed that I wasn't pregnant; and he obliged me.

The lady doctor had told me that, from the way I was feeling, I very likely was pregnant: Hadn't I been married two months? she said. Hadn't my periods stopped? Wasn't I being sick first thing in the morning? Yes, but I knew in my own mind that that first unsatisfactory business – we were both tired and weary, my nose was bleeding again and he had flu – could never have produced a child. Hence, the navy relic.

No, I wasn't going to have a baby, he said; my trouble was a stopped bowel. And he attended me three times a week for two months trying to get rid of the stopped bowel: he injected me with something which he assured me had been the last thing to come out of France, no chance of getting any more until the war was over. On behalf of all the pregnant women of St Albans at that time I can say, thank God for that.

At the end of two months he sat by my bed and held my hand and informed me in a whisper that I was pregnant. The last stuff to have come out of France hadn't done the trick, although it had taken everything out of me apparently except my brains, and the foetus.

I recall thinking of all the ships being sunk at that time, but there HE was sitting on the end of my bed smiling at me.

He started to discuss cosmetics again, the basis of which, he told me, was lanolin. 'Use raw lanolin,' he said, 'pure lanolin.'

I did and I stank like a sheep pen.

He might have done me incalculable harm because at six months I lost my baby; and yet I think I would have lost it in any case, for I was Rhesus-negative, which term, I now understand, wasn't known then; and also that my blood trouble was an inherited vascular disease called telangiectasia.

I can laugh about all my doctor episodes with the exception of one; this still rankles with bitterness. After being neglected by this particular doctor for years and putting up with the neglect so as not to cause trouble, at the end of a two months' illness during which I had been bleeding heavily and had not been visited but had been told over the phone to pack myself with iron, raw liver and hog's blood, of which, being allergic to them, I could take only small quantities, my husband committed the unprecedented crime of asking this particular doctor to visit me on a Saturday afternoon, and only then because our neighbour who had looked at me lying inert had said, 'You send for the doctor, Saturday or no Saturday, or she won't last long.' Tom was even worse than I when it comes to troubling someone.

When the reluctant doctor at last sat by my bed the conversation went as follows: 'What's the matter with you?'

'I feel ill. Tom says I've had pneumonia and I think it's the exhaustion from loss of blood . . . I've been bleeding a lot. I don't know, I just feel ill.'

'You should take iron.'

'I take as much as I can.'

'Do you know, I have patients over seventy years old, one or two nearly eighty, and they will never let me go and visit them. They always make their way to the surgery and some of them are really ill. Oh, but they do have . . .'

A long, long pause while I stared at this doctor and took in this parable. I couldn't believe it.

'Are you meaning to say that . . . that I haven't any gumption?'

'Well, yes, I think you're lacking a little . . .'

I was very low mentally and physically. I had been bleeding for weeks and had had a specialist to visit me, only to tell me nothing could be done for the bleeding as it was hereditary: when I bled I should have to go to bed and remain still. If that was the prescribed treatment, then I should have been in bed since I was eighteen. But now, through my depleted frame, there swept like a sheet of flame a deep anger against this injustice.

There were numerous things in life to which I could not lay claim: a name of my own, except that acquired through marriage, a university education, and a healthy body, but there was one thing I thought I possessed and that was the quality called gumption. In my low state and rising wrath against this person I was unable to quell a bout of self-pity and so asked myself: What but gumption had brought me from William Black Street to where I was at this moment, an established writer? What but gumption had lifted Katie McMullen from service at fourteen, from a laundry checker at eighteen to manageress at twenty-two, then, at the age of twenty-seven, into the gentleman's residence in Hoadswood Road, and this accomplished without any *man* behind her? What had given her the education necessary to transfer her racing imagination to paper? Perhaps it took no gumption to read and study after an eight-hour day in the laundry and four hours in putting a guest-house to rights for the following day. And what was the power that helped her to fight a breakdown that took ten long years in its ebbing? And what name could be given to the continual fighting against the depleting effects of telangiectasia?

You have no gumption! I have been hurt many times during my life but I don't think anything has hit me as hard as this.

The anger brought me out of the depths and it flamed out of me in spluttering spurts and sent this doctor hurrying from the room, to say to my husband, 'I think I've upset her.'

Later, when I was in the North to give a talk and spoke of this to a doctor friend, I ended by saying, 'I know that doctors are overworked and very busy,' and he, a doctor and a consultant, cut in with, 'If they're overworked they're getting paid for it and a doctor's presence at a patient's bedside is to reassure him, or her, and bring them comfort; it may not always be with a bedside manner but that should be his prime objective because the comfort or reassurance is a great part of the cure.'

As I've said elsewhere there are good doctors, good priests, and good dustmen.

Leave Me This

Take all else from me but leave me this:
Courage in the hours of the night to face the
mind,
Courage to face the long black day of the
blind,
Courage of the maimed with no fingers to
write,
Courage of the neurotic with his battle to
fight,
Courage of the lonely one behind his mask;
Courage, courage, and more courage, this is
what I ask:
Courage of the coward, often the bravest of
all,
Courage to laugh at lost fame as I fall,
Courage of the sick with no hope of reprieve,
Courage of the persistent who will never
achieve,
Courage that hope brings from the eternal
breast,
Courage to face, smiling, my last long rest.

ALL OUR HELLS

$\int_{0}^{3}$

For some time now I've re-
alised I am not going to hell; there's no need, for it's right
here, inside me.

As I see it, we don't go to hell, we haven't to move an
inch out of ourselves. All the material which goes towards
its making is within us and, consequently, in using our free
will we make our own hells with our thinking. And there's
no hell to equal a self-made hell. There are hells that others
make for us but they haven't the breaking power of those
whose structures we ourselves create.

For years I've been trying to cultivate the power of
thought, for I am convinced that it is this power which,
when controlled, can erase not only the traditional idea of
hell, which, strange as it may seem in this day of enlighten-
ment some of us still fearfully believe in, but also the more
potent self-made one.

The more you use this power constructively in thoughts
of courage and faith in oneself the stronger you gradually
feel yourself becoming, and you stop being kicked around
by those thoughts which accompany depression, and
worry, and sick anxiety.

It is a marvellous feeling when you realise you have
power over your thought, not it over you. But this power,
like most things worthwhile, makes a demand, and the
demand is THAT YOU USE IT, HOURLY, DAILY;
while sleeping and waking YOU MUST USE IT.

Years ago, my husband when in bed used to bump his

head three times on the pillow just before going to sleep and say, 'Seven o'clock. Seven o'clock. Seven o'clock.' And he would wake promptly at seven. He never used an alarm clock. This little trick of auto-suggestion led me to put it to my own use. Before dropping off to sleep, I would imagine myself being charged with courage, because oh, how I needed courage, and I knew courage was the antithesis of fear. I had learned not to plead and yammer, 'Oh God, take away this fear,' but to say firmly instead, 'I have courage,' and I would imagine I could actually see it pouring down into my sleeping body, burning up the fears in my mind, filling it with new life.

But don't let me glamorize this. Nothing happens overnight. Fears take years to grow to full maturity, and the point at which they take you over completely is termed a breakdown, so you can't get rid of overnight what in many cases has taken thirty years to grow. Yet what utter relief you experience when one day you suddenly find yourself on top and you know that you have a weapon with which to attack your fears. And strangely, it is the same weapon that brought them into being, simply your thinking.

Now, you might be saying that if thought can do such marvellous things why can't we free ourselves in the long run from illnesses? I'm not God, I can't answer that one, I can only say that right hopeful thinking can in some cases act like a miracle; especially is it invaluable to those of us troubled with nerves, for it will eventually alter our whole outlook towards this scourge.

Perhaps it is because my life has been a fight, a secret fight every inch of the way, that I have come to think nothing is lasting unless you fight for it. A number of us wonder why things don't work out for us: other people seem to find peace of mind, health and happiness but it doesn't come our way. Do you know something? I think it is because we don't DEMAND that these things should be ours. Now don't sit there and say, 'Hot air! She's talking through her hat.' I wish that years ago I had stood my ground instead of snivelling and in no small voice cried, 'I'm not going to put up with this constant fear, this feeling of guilt and shame because of my birth, to hell with it! The Kingdom of God, so I'm told, is within me. All right, then this being so I can do anything I put my mind to.'

If I'd done that in my thirties I'd have saved myself a breakdown in my forties and at least three of the seven complaints I'm stuck with now.

Time and again I've yelled at the Almighty, this Headmaster of Men, and demanded to know, Why me? Yes; why me? Who planned my destiny anyway? Who cut its pattern? Why was I sent to such a hard school, full of battle and strife to learn the lessons of life? Why was my ambition thwarted in the first place when my will was strong to succeed? Why was my body made weak when my spirit yearned to climb the heights? Why? my mind demanded over the years.

Time and again, I've talked this over with Tom; and one day, the schoolmaster in him replied, 'Well, perhaps it's the kind of exam the Headmaster of Men sets for those special pupils in His form.'

As we grow older we all come to see God in different ways. This is how I see Him.

> *God has no denomination,*
> *He enters into no category,*
> *Catholic, Protestant, Mohammedan or Jew;*
> *God is the love you have inside,*
> *The strength, the courage*
> *To abide by what to you is true;*
> *He is the joy you feel with the wondrous*
>   *dawn,*
> *The mystery of spring*
> *The compassion for animals in pain,*
> *The giving of yourself without thoughts of*
>   *gain;*
> *He is the understanding of a stranger's plight;*
> *He is courage in the grip of fear;*
> *He is the power to like yourself*
> *And cultivate traits*
> *You hold dear in others;*
> *He is the dictionary*
> *Who gives you the meaning of good.*

Life is so short. If only in old age we were given another life in which to carry out what we have learned in this; but no, we have to face up to the fact that our span is brief. The only comfort, if it can be so called, is that it is the same for every human of every race. So how, I've asked myself, do I live it? And when I go what shall I find? Will it be heaven or hell? In my case, I'd say neither, for I cannot take my life with me, for in it I would have left both my heaven and hell behind.

GOING BACK

When, in 1945, I returned to Hastings there were lots of things I told myself I would never do again, and one of them was pick up a pencil. The very sight of a pencil could put my nerves on a jangling edge. The intricate work that I had done with it had certainly brought my nerves to breaking point.

My life at this time was bleak. I wanted colour. So one day, on impulse, I took my paints and went out into the garden where poppies were growing amid the mass of weeds that had propagated themselves during our five years' absence, and I painted the first poppy picture featured in this book. I did not paint another flower for thirty-one years.

Following the poppies I did try to paint a scene in the garden, but it was a mess; then with my second effort, which took place indoors, I became dizzy and ill from the smell of the turps, and also the white lead in the paint revived the effects of the lead poisoning I'd contracted from two years of pen painting in my teens. So that outlet was closed to me forever; or so I thought.

We moved North from Hastings in 1976 and we hadn't been in our new house in Corbridge more than a few months when, of a sudden, I had the overpowering desire to paint, and of all things, the sea.

Now I had lived within a stone's throw from the seafront for quite some time of my first two years in Hastings, then for the rest of the forty-six years never more than two miles away, and never a week passed in the early days that I did not walk along that seafront.

I recall that during my first few months in Hastings I walked most nights from the fish market right to the bathing pool in St Leonards and back, which, I think, is a distance of at least two miles each way, because I was very lonely. Sometimes I would sit and listen to the band but most times I just walked. Not only did I like the exercise but also I felt I needed it after eight hours spent in the atmosphere of a laundry.

One night in particular I recall vividly. It was extremely hot; the moon was coming up over the sea; the beach was strewn with people lying about trying to keep cool. The couples canoodling under the promenade wall added to my feeling of loneliness. But at one point I stood for a long time looking out to sea. The moon had buried itself deep in the water. I had never seen such a beautiful sight. And it was that scene I recalled when the urge came upon me once again to paint.

My first attempt had no softness in it. I hadn't known what I was going to do when I started on that canvas, but it ended up in a great curling wave. Yet the following two I painted were of quiet night scenes. I did ten altogether, one after the other. Of course, they took me some time because I was able to afford to give them only small stints stolen from my writing. But how strange it was that after forty-six years I should want to paint memories of the sea at Hastings, and that it should give me pleasure, because many of my memories of that time certainly weren't pleasurable. I think the big angry wave might have given vent to that feeling.

KNOWLEDGE THROUGH PAIN

〜

There is a period in my life that I look back upon as the time my spirit was born. In a way it was like another breakdown, and for a while I had such a keen awareness of life that it became agonising; it was as if I had been stripped of my skin and all the emotions were pricking the raw flesh.

After years of searching, after years of nights when my last thought had been to suggest peace of mind, after years of trying to find a crutch in another church, after years of reading and discussion with Tom, I arrived at this stage of awareness in life.

The truth is different for each individual, but for me it came in the knowledge that there is an impartial power that is no less in the tiger-nut than in the tiger, the same power that is in a maggot is in man. I saw the power passing through and interlacing all things: from the worm, going into the bird; from the meat going into man, from the plankton into the whale, and from the whale into the oil, and the oil into a thousand uses; from the dead flesh or the ashes of man into beast, bird, and tree, through bricks and mortar, through atoms and molecules, I knew this power to be linked.

As it passed through me I felt that I could conserve and master it, much or little according to the strength of my desire and will. My ego glowed with this knowledge.

I had always been aware of pain, the pain endured by people, the pain endured by children and animals, oh yes, this latter is a very keen awareness, the pain endured by children and dumb animals. But this new awareness went beyond humans and animals to the very source of life. I ached with this pain whenever I saw anyone snapping off the head of a flower, or catching a butterfly; I cringed inside when I swatted a fly, even going as far as apologising to it for bringing its life span to an end. This was the reason for my pain, when you cut the life force it was finished.

So I thought at the time, and reasoned that if there were another existence in which the life force could flourish once more then my pain would have been without purpose.

At this stage I asked myself, Was life normal for me? And the answer was, What is meant by normal? All I am sure of now is that at that time I was experiencing as it were the labour pains of the birth of my spirit, and it was far from being an enviable process. I was being given an insight in a way to the Power and the Glory and, as marvellous as that sounds, I wouldn't want to experience that period again – ever.

But I am grateful for the knowledge it has brought me, for I know I am not just flesh, blood and brain – I have within me something that can reach out and touch as it were the intangible God.

Pain

Tom started a migraine at four o'clock this morning, it is now midnight. He is sitting propped up in the dark in the study. He can never lie down when he's in this state and if he moves his head before the attack has worn itself out it could start all over again.

I always feel so helpless at such times. I look at his eyes, the water's streaming from them like tears of agony. I long to be able to do something. I can help myself in illness, I have even on one or two occasions been able to help others, but for this man, who means everything to me, I can do nothing, only look on.

> *Rivets drilled through eyes.*
> *Temples beaten like Indian brass.*
> *Stomach riving in sickness.*
> *Brain not dulled by the battery*
> *Of blood in swollen veins*
> *Sends its proof through lids*
> *Oozing their essence of pain*
> *Migraine.*

Insomnia

Dawn breaking:
Light like steel grey paint
Slithers down the window
And drags back the curtain on day,
Day that I've longed for
Through each black hour
When wide-eyed I've stared
at fear and watched
It grow
Like a weed in compost
And felt its tendrils
Strangle my courage
Until, brought low,
I weep for day,
For in the light
I can sleep.

The Lonely One

The room is filled with noise:
Chatter, laughter, bursts of song;
I hunch my shoulders against the roar.
People are flooding in,
Pushing at each other at the door.
A Happy New Year.
A Happy New Year.
Here's to us!
Hello there! Why, hello there!
Faces I haven't seen since yesteryear.
They pass between me and the firelight.
Deprived of warmth, I shiver.
The hubbub fades;
The chatter, the laughter, and bursts of song
Seep into the silence and are gone.
But the silence remains;
I still have that;
And the single bed,
The table,
And the knick-knacks,
And the radio chat.

Barren

The secret pain
The quiet pain
The riving pain
Of jealousy
That brings no gain
For barren womb
From which no seed
Will breed
And on a cry
Struggle to life
And grow to joy
Or strife
A boy
Or daughter fair
Companion
Down the growing and ageing years.

What compensation then?
Only such comfort
As it gives
You can afford.
Answerable
For self alone
To God.

Loss

Happiness is the seed bed of pain
That generates sorrow.

I was happy in my love.
Tomorrow I knew must come
And tears would rain
And my heart would bleed.
If I had not craved happiness
I would have been inured
Against sorrow;
But life does not warn the heart
That from the joyish height
The fall is great,
And the seedling of love
Is now a sword
And tomorrow has come.

Why did I not accept today?

A ROSE BY ANY OTHER NAME

As I have said before, if there is anything after death it will be a great adventure; if not, then just one long dreamless sleep. And who would not welcome a dreamless sleep?

When I think that we may be born again through reincarnation, then I become worried that I may not return in the person I've come to know during this particular span. I can manage her . . . up to a point. But say I were to return in another's body that was possessed of evil. Well now, that terrifies me, for I have a big enough job to keep the dark impulses of this *me* under control.

You know, the devil is always presented as if he were amused or laughing, and as a big handsome man, isn't he? I've often wondered about this, as I've wondered too about the popular image of Christ, this tall, clean, perfect featured Adonis who looks too good to be true.

Why do we always demand perfect physique to represent the epitome of power and strength, when history down the ages has been altered by beings of small or medium height and of no particular beauty? Napoleon, Hitler, Mussolini, these well-known representatives of power in small frames, and all with enlarged egos.

And now the latest discovery: Christ, it is being stated, was a small and even ugly man. Can you take it? I find it hard. Yet just think back to the days when he lived, and place in them a working man, a carpenter, a Jew. From where do we get our white-robed, pale-faced Adonis?   -

If God did send His Son down to earth, then surely He'd have the sense to know He'd have a better chance to get under a man's skin if He didn't stick out like a sore thumb and appear so high in all ways above them that he would be impossible to follow.

I, myself, cannot imagine what He looked like; that was known only to a few. The only thing I know is that many of his sayings ring true even in this sophisticated age, but nevertheless they're still very hard to live up to.

But does our conception of His face or His physique really matter? After all, it is simply His grace that we seek.

Morning Prayer

Let me, oh Lord, this day
Make someone happy
By what I do
Or what I say
And when my thoughts
To irritation roam
Lord let me remember
Charity begins at home.
– – Towards HIM
MY IN-LAWS
And the bairns
And the countless chores
– – – And oh lor!
– Not forgetting her next door.

FRIENDSHIP

Now, I am fully aware of my bad points; also a number of points I had not considered bad until kind friends pointed them out to me as such. What I want and need, though, from any friend is not censure but bucking up. I want my few good points brought to the fore; I want to know that they're noticed and liked. This won't tend towards fostering conceit, as is often supposed; it will, in my case, give me self-confidence and poise, make me feel more friendly towards myself . . . which is a very important feeling . . . and consequently it will make me more friendly to others, for, you know, you can only give out what you have in.

Some people think that because they are on friendly terms with you it gives them licence to point out all the little things that annoy them and which, they imagine, annoy others. Very often the bad points they stress so much in me . . . and you . . . are their own main faults. Like a friend who kept me on the phone for half an hour one morning, telling me of her journey up to London, of her buying clothes, of the wonderful lunch she'd had at a posh restaurant, of doing a show; on and on, only to say, the next day, in front of a number of people, 'Oh! Kitty would talk the hind legs off a donkey.'

Of course, this is only a light example of what I mean. But some of the holes that these friends feel it their duty to pick in one can lead, in the case of a sensitive person, to needless painful introspection.

When, at some time in your life, you are pitched into the

barren wastes and desolation of your own soul, and this happens at least once in a lifetime to most of us; when you are probing, and questioning, and crying: Is there a God? If so, why this? or that? . . . or even, WHY AM I HERE AT ALL? If, at this time, there is someone to whom you can fly, as I once did years ago, and get the answer to my high-falutin gabbling about the desolation of my soul, then you'll be lucky, for what she said was: 'Aw, sit yerself down, hinny, and have a cup of tea. Look! try this yeasty-cake; it's just out of the oven. It'll likely give you indigestion, but you'll enjoy it . . . And move that jar of flowers out of your way; the bairns tramped into the country to get them for me . . . Hasn't it been a grand day? The sun's been shining on the backyard wall for hours; it makes you glad you're alive . . . Now, what were you saying about the desolation of your soul, hinny? Eeh! such high-falutin words you come out with. You're a clever lass.'

That may sound very corny today, simplicity often does, but on that day her words met my need before I'd opened my mouth further. She could hardly crawl around her tiny kitchen for rheumatism; she was a prisoner within four walls and a backyard. But, not unthinking, she offered to the barren waste that really was myself at that moment three things: food, flowers, and sunshine. Three things which gave her happiness she handed to me. So penetrating was her simplicity that when I left her later I thought there must be something within her to make her think like that and to be happy in that cramped cheerless environment.

A long time has passed and that old lady is now dead, but I always remember her, for she was . . . a friend, and true friends are few and far between. You can have hundreds of acquaintances, but if you have three staunch friends you are lucky, for you know their ears and hands will be there when you need them. Such a pair of hands belong to my husband, and during one of my dark periods I said to him in so many words:

Give me your hand to help me on my way;
Give me your hand to get me through this
  day;
Give me your hand to face up to life;
Give me your hand to clasp in the night
When dreams bring fears more real than day;
Give me your hand to let me know I'm not
  alone.
Don't wait for an anniversary to tell me that
  you care,
    Without your hand now, when that
      comes I may not be there.

Give me your hand to soothe the wounds of
  life
That I cannot wash away with tears;
Give me your hand that I can cling to down
  the years,
And when I near the end and my path is
  stony with pain,
Let it be there to grasp firmly
As I take the dark bend to walk down that
  unknown lane.

TREES

I was twenty-three when I first went to the South of England and I lived there for forty-six years, and for forty-three of them I was surrounded by trees, and just as some people talk to flowers I talked to the trees.

But this form of communication didn't come about until my illness in 1945. I think one must be in need of spiritual help or have experienced some form of travail before one really becomes aware of the power, strength and sympathy that can be imbibed from a tree.

I first experienced the power one dark day, mentally dark. I was walking in our bit of woodland and I remember the exact words that at the time were galloping through my fear-filled, tormented mind. They were, 'Oh God! what am I going to do? I can't go on any longer like this.'

Unconsciously I had stopped near an oak tree and I leant my brow against it as if I were going to beat my head on it; then I turned round and pressed my back tight against the trunk, my palms flat on the bark; and slowly I felt the tension slipping from me, draining from me and into the ground, and it was as if the tree was saying to me, 'Breathe deeply,' for I let out a long-drawn sigh, then began to inhale slowly.

This was the beginning of a relationship between the oaks and me. Strangely, there would be periods of time during which I would forget about the therapeutic effects of the trees; these would be when I was feeling able to cope; but whenever I went down I would say to myself, go into the wood, and always when I did I got some measure of help.

Some would say it was merely auto-suggestion. Well, if it was, it was instigated by the oak tree in the first place.

When in '54 we moved to 'Loreto' we partly cleared more than two acres of woodland in order to make a garden, and never once did a tree fall but I felt go through me a pang, touching on sorrow.

There is one thing I've missed since coming back to the North, and that is the big trees. I see them in other people's gardens but not in my own, and so we have started to plant trees and my hope is that in the years to come someone will stand with his back to one of the trees and know that he's in touch with nature's doctor.

> I thank you oak
> For being a friend
> Against whom I could lay my head
> And embrace you in my need.
> In the autumn,
> When I swept your myriad acorns
> That urged to sprout your seed
> I knew, in shame, come the spring,
> I'd uproot them by the score
> And, what was more,
> Curse the labour of the chore.
> Yet, here and there,
> I'd leave a
> Strongly spurting youngster
> To flourish and grow,
> For in the years to come,
> When it was of a size,
> Some head would lean against it
> And recognise
> Peace, likewise.

I Am Alive

Under a tree,
Clouds of green above me,
Bark and sap
At my back,
Heels in soil,
I resist toil
And thoughts of hell
Or heaven
Or war that I wished for yesterday
To soak up
Skin-heads
And louts
And students
With their periodic
Bouts
Of stressing the I.
Here would I lie
For ever
If the sun remained still
And will that all things be
For ever
As now;
For I do not in this
Moment strive
To prove I am alive,
I am alive.

Melancholy

On this day with sunshine mellow
And the trees taking their last fling
In russet, gold and brown,
Why should my heart be heavy?
Am I afraid that like nature
I'll be drawn into the earth bed
Of desolate sleep,
But, unlike it, there for me
Shall be no spring,
No bursting forth with renewed life
In my ageing bones,
No power to move my arms
And embrace the wind,
To turn my face up to the rain
Or deck myself for summer once again?
The final death of a tree
Is mush or smoke;
How fortunate it doesn't know its end.
Humanity pays for its numbered springs
In realising what its autumn brings.

The Cycle

The wood is the world,
Brown, yellow, white, and black,
All begot heedlessly from drifting pollen,
Or thrust by bees, instinct guided
From slime forgotten time,
And in darkness breaking the womb of the
*   soil,*
Sucked upwards into light
To imagine rose blush and beech fire,
Endless eternity made for their blooming.
How sad is autumn in the wood.
No use to say the seed is sown again
And life is springing.
What comfort to the dying another birth.

Peace

Sunday morning on the lawn;
No church bell splitting the air
Beckoning me to prayer,
To give thanks for the corn
Of my daily bread,
Or to confess my guilt,
In which process I wilt
And wish that I were dead.

In the lawn grows a tree,
That is God to me.

STRIFE

A breakdown is like the eruption of a volcano. Your mind is boiling with the most terrifying thoughts, all negative, fear, aggressiveness, hate, self-pity; they come spewing up, spilling over, overpowering you for a time. But just as a volcano gradually wears itself out, so your mind settles, at least on the surface. It might take weeks or months or, as in my case, years before the fire in the embers finally cools down. Even then, little pockets keep flaring up. A domestic upset or, again as in my case, overwork and ill health, and there you are, petrified that you are in for another bout. Yet through practice I have learned how to escape my particular gorge of despair, for I tell myself emphatically I have only to use the bulldozer of hope on it and it will go.

It sounds so simple, but it has become so only after a great deal of practice. Hope is the only equipment that gets me out of the gorge and up the mountain. Hope that tomorrow I'll be myself again. TOMORROW – never today. That's another thing I've had to learn. Hope never materialises today. It only comes tomorrow, and even then it has got to be fought for, striven for.

That word striven, or strive, is a hard word. I remember at one stage crying out against it because I was so tired of strife. I remember asking why I couldn't be like other people, have a little joy, happiness, peace of mind. Oh, I wanted peace of mind. Life, I felt, owed me this after what I'd gone through.

Well, as always when I asked a straight question of myself I usually got a straight answer, and the answer was, Why not strife? For at this stage of my age I had to realise that the only wisdom I had gleaned had been sucked from strife. Fighting through fear, sickness, and pain which, in the main were the result of strife, had taught me that a life of any worth was bred on such strife; it had been a kind of yeast in my case which had brought me to an understanding and an awareness of the strength within me, the spirit within me, and that it was only through strife, and striving, my hope would materialise tomorrow.

January 18th, 1975

I felt very ill yesterday. The feeling continued into the night; I couldn't sleep. My Siamese twin, self-pity, was in charge. This was a real bout of mental exhaustion. For months now it has been a fourteen-hour day, seven days a week, up at half-past six in the morning trying to get through my ever growing mail; the day allotted to the phone, visits from agents, editors, photographers, interviewers and, just recently, the BBC unit. I tell myself it can't go on, but it does.

Lying there last night in the dark with Tom by my side I asked myself what I wanted, and strangely the answer was — joy.

Lord, beckon me to joy;
My mind is weary,
My body sick,
Who can I employ
To ease my spirit
And lift my heart

STRIFE

And give me strength
To combat this strife
And the energy
To work at life?
Lord, beckon me to joy.

I have no hobbies;
No more do I knit,
Play the piano, or paint;
My mind abhors the needle,
My fingers irritate the keys;
I see no colours, no trees.

Then what do I do
With my days?
I write.
And part of the night
My pen I employ.

Lord, oh Lord,
If you are there
Answer my prayer:
Give me joy.

Dreams
What Are We Really?

With the light I clutch at dreams
Sliding back into the night
In an effort to view more closely
Which side of me is right:
I, staid and sober,
My pen poised probingly?
Or the other,
That can act so mad and foolishly?

Did I in my dreams
Actually fly naked over Kew
To land in the Palace Yard
Astride a horse
And find myself
In full armour of course?
Did I punch and beat my mother,
Then see myself in an open dale
So beautiful as to take the breath,
Only to find it a prison
Ringed with walls
And myself fighting to escape,
As if from death?

My dreams are rarely happy.
Which is me?
Am I who write, the phantasy
And she in dreams, reality?
If when I die I dream in death,
Then I shall know.

For my eightieth birthday Doctor Brian Enright, the Newcastle University librarian, presented me with a book. It was an old book but in pristine condition. It had been compiled by three men in 1850, the poetry by R. A. Bacon, designs by Owen Jones and the drawing on stone by E. L. Bateman. The result of all this was twelve paintings depicting fruits from gardens and fields. Among them was a painting of an apple, another of a peach, one of strawberries, and one of cherries. It is a beautiful and unusual book. And I wondered if I could copy one of the plates, but the entwined flowers and fruit I saw as a daunting task. Yet, as Tom says, I always start at the hardest end of everything first.

Well, there's the result in the colour section. They were achieved with almost literally a single-haired brush. There were four hairs in it to begin with. As I have only partial sight I had to make use of a magnifying glass; and this, I found at times very frustrating and irritating, and was for giving up after painting the apple, until Tom said I shouldn't attempt the strawberries, they were much too difficult . . . He certainly knows what he's doing: I finished the strawberries and started on the cherries.

SUSPENDED TIME

I sat thinking today of the spark that sets the seal of greatness on a mind. My thoughts went back to Richard Church's *A Window On a Hill*, from the reading of which I had been given various leads: a quoted line of poetry which I felt I must explore further; a reference to a town I must visit later; intimate talks about numbers of men, their doings, their books and their sayings, and about whom it became imperative I should know more. Yet although I felt I loved this book, this man, and his knowledge, it left me strangely depressed; I had been in touch with someone who seemed possessed of a bottomless store of wisdom.

Perhaps it was a feeling of jealousy that came over me, for I possess no great wisdom and very little real knowledge. I am filled only with an urgent groping, a desire to know, and an irritation caused by the time taken up in daily tasks that swamp my thinking and suck my high thoughts into the vortex of wasted time. Yet, oh how I want to be wise; to clutch and hold the evasive wisps of the meaning of being that breathes itself into life at the birth of sleep and floats into death on my awakening.

I long to put into words the essence of the quietness that settles upon me at odd moments; but at such times I do not fly for my pen, for then I do not want 'to do', I only want 'to be'; and I know dimly in these moments, that no greater knowledge can come to me than what I manage to hold consciously in that suspended time, and in that time I feel that the sum of all knowledge is but recognition of THAT MOMENT, and that THAT MOMENT is all there is, and so filled with exquisite peace that you long to spread it over into an hour, a day, a lifetime.

Such odd moments are few and far between and so I long desperately for their return and, what is more important, to try to contain their essence.

But I was speaking of Richard Church and his *A Window On A Hill*, and I return to it and garner, like a hungry peasant, the harvest of his mind so liberally sown through the pages, and as I read I know that it takes men such as he to translate those odd moments that elude us. We go to our own particular church to find them; we enter into silences hoping to find them; I myself resolved to be a better person, thinking that, in gracious payment, some Deity will bestow them more frequently upon me so that my life henceforth will be a tranquil, fear-free oasis. But through my very striving I defeat myself, for these moments are gifts, presents from the Gods, so to speak. Golden moments when the pages of a book open to reveal a light, like a candle in the night, so bright it illuminates the mind but at the same time prompts you to probe and ask the eternal *Whys*: Why suffering? Why death? – until the candle guts and the snuffer of your mind extinguishes the light, and you're in the dark again and you know there is no answer. There never has been, and never will be; the only solution is acceptance of the fact that we are not to know.

Time

The galloping grasshopping moments of
    thought
Recalling, delving, raking the past,
Reviving sediments of sorrow,
Reliving the dregs of affection long lost,
Wasting the present, at what cost to the
    future,
The short, short future
No matter how long,
Wherein this fleeting space
Imagined, caught now, experienced, held,
Will in one flashing second of existence
Be merged for eternity
In time past.

Meditate and Contemplate

With a mind like mine
That leaps from earth to star,
Rides back to earth on lightning
To bury deep into the volcano's bed,
Where the thought is burnt out
Faster than the blaze from a laser,
And I am left, not sadly bereft of the
    knowledge,
But vitally aware
That I can neither
Meditate nor contemplate

Yet I can concentrate;
How other could I write
And probe the mercury of my mind;
My brain is not blind,
Yet it fails to construe
What is needed
To sink into the peace
Of meditation or contemplation.

HOPE AND PAIN

∽

1960 was another very
tough year for me; one ailment after another was hitting
me. I had a struggle to keep working. The residue of the
breakdown would rear its head every now and again and I
was at a low ebb. But when you hit bottom there's no way
out but up.

I remember the day I left the bottom. I was standing at
the window looking out on to the wood, and there arose in
me a wave of anger and I cried to myself, 'I will have peace
of mind . . . I will! I may have to go through greater
mental strife yet, but some day I shall walk in quiet places
and know peace.'

I believe in auto-suggestion. I believe that if you want a
thing badly enough you will get it. I believe in casting your
bread upon the waters, so to speak, and from that time
onwards I cast my bread, in the form of hope, on the water
every day. It might only be a crumb, but I threw it out on
to the waves of thought.

That, as I said, was in 1960.

Now, in 1978, and for the past six or seven years, I have
known peace of mind and spirit such as I had never
imagined possible. I don't go to any church, I don't pray
. . . but I think, and when I think along certain lines I am in
tune with the power that, for a better name, is called God.

Spiritually at least I have come a long way since my
breakdown in 1945, and I have still some way to go yet,
and I'm still asking questions, about pain for instance.

113

Now, I'd be the first to deny that any kind of pain is good, but pain is with us, all kinds of pain, pain of body, pain of mind and pain of spirit. Doctors and surgeons can ease some pains but there are others that go so deep into the mind that only you yourself can reach them: you are your own doctor, your own surgeon.

HOPE AND PAIN

Pain in muscle, bone, and brain
Deadens the heart and spirit
And asks, What is there to be gained
By living?

Nights when the depths are reached,
Day when the hours are breached
By pills and palliatives
And cheering remarks from friends:
Buck up now, buck up;
Take a pull at yourself,
You'll soon be well.

Go to hell! Go to hell!

Why me?
What have I done?
The question from self-pity runs;
And the answer never comes
– At least not as you expect –
With an instant ease,
But slowly on the spirit falls a light,
Faint, flickering, wavering,
A delicate thing
So fragile that you slant your gaze in fear
That it will take flight.

But it stays,
Becoming brighter with the days,
Until through its light
In wondrous calmness
You see a word,
Rejected by you
Through denominations and creeds
Yet sought through the hunger of your soul
And now shining in truth
Like a proven sword,
WHATEVER IS, IS GOD.

THE NEED FOR APPLAUSE

⌒

I once said my husband was a comfort to me in my success and was asked why anyone should need comfort in success. Well, it was like this.

When in 1950 my first book was published I experienced joy, ecstasy, slight delirium, and that understandable superior feeling that comes with the publication of a first novel. Yet some part of me still remained naïve for I imagined that everybody would joy with me; but to my amazement only a small percentage of my acquaintances, so-called friends, came up to my expectations. In fact, the main reaction to my success was silence.

I happened to belong to a small group of ladies who did good works making and collecting things for charity. So when the news broke that my first novel had been accepted I couldn't wait to get amongst them and be weighed down by their fulsome praise. I had rehearsed the attitude I must adopt when they fell about my neck: I was to be modest and deprecating of my immense intellectual powers.

On the night of the expected glory I sat for two and a half hours among them while the conversation ranged widely, from an absent friend whom they all agreed made herself sick only to get her husband's attention, through the six o'clock news, to the dizzy heights of finance when they debated the price one could put on a hand-made cosy, but not a word was said about Catherine Cookson's great achievement . . . And it was a great achievement. I had been scribbling since I was a child and there I was forty-four years old. I had fought and survived many personal wars, the latest being a mental one for I was then still suffering from a breakdown, and so I felt entitled to consider it an achievement.

I cried all the way home. Tom, always a comfort, said, 'They're jealous.'

Jealous? JEALOUS? Who among that crowd could be jealous of me? Hadn't one been to a university and was loaded with degrees? Had they not all benefited from private school education? I should delete the word benefited.

I felt I should never go back into their company again, but being a devil for punishment and with the hope that perhaps they really hadn't heard of my success I joined them once more.

Again I walked home howling my eyes out.

Perhaps it was a good thing this happened because their attitude, which was repeated when later I made my first broadcast, together with the reaction of our baker, firmly nailed my feet to the ground, and there they have remained over the past thirty-six years.

With regard to our baker. He was a very tall man, a superior type. I sometimes thought he might have been an officer in the army and had come down to the baker's van. Anyway, he had little or nothing to say; we didn't even discuss the weather. But, of course, I can understand the man's attitude to me at that time for he must have thought me a bit odd. On his twice-weekly visits I would be in the garden, in all weathers, either sawing trees down and sawing them up, or digging, or raking, and when I saw him coming through the gateway, instead of calling out to him, 'The money and the order are on the draining board, baker,' I would do a kind of tick-tack which must have puzzled him as, undoubtedly, would have my whole appearance.

You see, our house was known as a gentleman's residence but my attire when working was anything but that of a lady. When you had to keep fifteen large rooms clean, cook, and wash . . . by hand, there wasn't much time left to dress up. It's amazing to me now how I fitted in my writing.

Anyway, when one morning the postman brought me my six free copies of *Kate Hannigan* there followed delirium pure and simple. At the time my sister-in-law happened to be staying with us and I read out to her bits that had been written by this 'very clever lass'. After a half-hour she had heard more than enough and she went out. And there I was left with this great achievement and with no one to listen to my talking about it.

Tom used to come in at half-past twelve for his lunch. Now, he had never patted me on the back and told me what a clever lass I was; no, he had criticized my work to an extent that at times reduced me to tears, but the moment he saw that book his reactions were the same as mine. He wanted to show it to someone, talk to somebody about it; he seemed to think it was no use talking to me for I knew about it.

It was at that moment that the baker happened to pass the window, and on the sight of him Tom exclaimed, 'I'll show it to the baker!'

I was horrified. 'You'll what!' I hissed. '*You'll not* . . . he thinks I'm doolally; he doesn't even give me the time of day.'

Now during the years we had been married I had learned that Tom suffered from the short man's complex, which means that he's got a growth, it's his ego, it's enlarged, it's all of six-foot-six. Knowing this, why was I fool enough to hiss at him again. 'You'll not! You'll not show it to that man.'

I can see him now actually putting two inches on to his five-foot-four-and-a-half as he stared at me; and then he said slowly, 'If I wish to show it to the baker I'll show it to the baker.' And on this he marched to the door and there, holding the book aloft he exclaimed, 'Look, baker, my wife's first novel!'

The baker looked at Tom; then he looked back at the

book, and very slowly, his eyes travelling to where I was standing, he said, 'WHITE OR BROWN?'

Success

Let your head soar
Let your dreams have air
Let them spread far into the future
Let them stir your heart
Let them in riches abound
– But keep your feet on the ground.

Let praises sing in your ears
Let reviews be as balm on your ego
Let success give you a feeling of power
Let adulation like music sound
– Only keep your feet on the ground.

Remembering always that what goes up must by Newton's 'Law of Gravity' come down.

Perhaps the only way to reach the stars is to come down to earth.

NERVES

$\backsim$

Until the beginning of the last war I had paid no attention to nerves. I knew people had nerves; I also knew people had leprosy; I knew as much about the one as about the other, but working at two jobs for ten years without a holiday and carrying an abnormal load of worry alone, then getting married and losing four babies prematurely during the war, and all the while being ashamed of my birth and early upbringing, besides a religious conflict, told on me both mentally and physically. The result was a nervous breakdown, and the losing of the use of my legs for a time and the absolute loss of self-confidence and faith and hope for a longer period.

Now only those who have gone through this hell know what it is like; no amount of putting yourself in the other fellow's place can bring you within leagues of it. Over the past years, however, nerves have become the scourge of men and women, and so, unfortunately, you may not find it necessary to have to put yourself in the other fellow's shoes.

I tried everything that might help me pull myself together, nothing was too small or silly sounding. I read every book that had been written on nerves and how to treat them. One I was diving into at that particular time told me to stress upon myself at all odd times of the day that I was perfectly well, there wasn't a thing the matter with me.

It sounded ridiculous, plain daft, because I knew I was ill, very ill, both mentally and physically. But I'd try anything once, anything to relieve my present state. At first I could keep it up for only a few minutes a day, sometimes not even that. I also tried to put it into practice whenever I was asked how I felt; instead of using that defeatist expression, I'm not feeling too good, I would force myself to answer, Oh, not too bad! and rarely, but sometimes, I would even manage to say, Oh, fine.

Gradually as time went on and I slowly improved, I was forced to face the fact that my type of nerves was caused not so much by my physical health as by my mental attitude.

If we could realise when we are young, and by young I mean in the twenties or early thirties, that much of our thinking is wrong, and that every negative thought is a step towards ill health, both physical and mental, we would, I am sure, make an effort to think straight. I know it wasn't so much what had happened to me since I was a child as how I thought about it, and worried about it during my twenties and thirties, that caused my breakdown.

The second game of pretence that the book suggested was to tell myself that I liked people. Oh, boy! this was a very difficult one. Be honest with yourself and think of the people you heartily dislike, and imagine willing yourself to like them. It isn't easy, is it? No, practically impossible. I can look back and laugh now at my efforts at this one.

You see, I had a neighbour who didn't like me, and I didn't like her. Their house was set higher than ours and through the upper clear part of our lavatory window you could see her path and back door, and so each morning I would adjourn to the small room at the time I knew she would be leaving home, to go to her work, and when I saw her coming out of the door I would prod myself . . . and mind I had to prod myself in order to make myself say, 'Good-morning, Mary.' That wasn't her name, but it'll do. 'Good-morning, Mary,' I'd mutter aloud. 'I hope you'll be happy and at peace today.' And invariably I would add, 'And when we meet you won't say anything nasty to me. God bless you, Mary.'

On my better days I would lean my head against the wall and giggle; on the days when I hated the world I would have to force good thoughts towards her through my teeth. Then perhaps that very night when we met socially there she would be, smiling at me whilst she would be cutting my throat with her bitchiness.

Oh, it's difficult to love some people. Anyway, this pretence game did, towards the end, pay off a little, for although I didn't become immune to what people said about me, or cry my eyes out at the jealousy directed towards me, I began to adopt a philosophical air towards people's reactions; and so in a way you could say it worked.

My third game was pretending to do something big. My bent had always been towards writing, so at that time I imagined myself writing a wonderful play and having it put on in London, and, of course, being there on the first night. I actually did write the play, and not only did I finish it but I wrote two others. They were never put on in London.

But later one of my books was made into a film, and I did have a 'first night' in London.

The next big thing I aimed at doing was to write a novel. How little did I think, when I started that novel, it would be the beginning of a career for me, and just at the time, too, when I thought life was too hard to cope with, and that I wasn't up to it and the best thing to do was to find a bridge or a river . . . or the equivalent.

A short time ago when speaking to a group of people I was asked a disconcerting question: Where did God come into my cure? It was disconcerting because although I had made no mention of prayer with regard to curing one's fears, it wasn't because I hadn't thought about it. As many of us know, with the loss of faith in life and in ourselves, faith in God goes too, and this is often accompanied by a great mental stress when prayer seems useless. I can say now what I said to that woman.

With one's readjusted values and the totally new outlook on life the fight with fear brings about comes a new conception of God and, as in my case, a new way of praying. I found that I could pray without using words; I found that I could approach God without going through intermediaries; I found that if I sat still and waited something spoke to me and told me what to do. Sometimes it was the voice of our Kate or of me granda, at other times it was a voice I didn't recognise.

God is as we imagine Him to be. Some of us imagine Him to be a figure-head, others see Him as a Power, an unseen force. But however we visualise Him, He has a voice, and if you sit quiet you'll hear it and your nerves and spirit will be eased.

The following lines helped me not only during the bad times but during the not so bad ones too, they helped me to keep on keeping on. I used to think I first saw them years ago in 'Happy Mag'. Perhaps I did, but recently when sorting a pile of old writings I found the original on a monthly calendar. I don't know the name of the author, but he or she certainly knew what he was talking about.

Believe This

You're winning. You simply cannot fail. The only obstacle is doubt; there's not a hill you cannot scale once fear is put to rout. Don't think defeat, don't talk defeat, the word will rob you of your strength. 'I will succeed.' This phrase repeat throughout the journey's length.

The minute that 'I can't' is said, you slam a door right in your face. Why not exclaim, 'I will' instead? Half won then is the race. You close the door to your success by entertaining one small fear. *Think happiness*, talk happiness, watch joy then coming near.

The word 'impossible' is black. 'I can' is like a flame of gold. No whining heart. Eyes! look not back; be strong, O Will, and bold. *You're winning though the journey's slow;* you're gaining steadily each day. Oh! Courage, what a warmth and glow you shed along the way.

THERE ARE DOCTORS
AND DOCTORS

∽

Although I have tried to throw off all the superstitions of my young days there still remains with me a deep potency of dreams. Any forthcoming illness out of the ordinary is told to me in the following manner.

At Christmas of 1969 I dropped into bed with the flu I had been fighting for days. I did not send for the doctor: we had been informed on the wireless not to trouble the doctors, everybody had flu.

It was towards the end of the second week when I was recovering that I had the dream. I found myself walking into a great black swamp and sank into slimy mud up to my knees. The feeling was dreadful, indescribable. I looked around me and as far as I could see there was nothing but this great flat layer of slime. Then a bank appeared and, stretching out from it into the slime, a wooden platform, and although this, too, was covered with slime I knew that once I reached it I could gain the bank; I also knew it would take me some time to lift my feet towards it.

I awoke in fear, and even the next morning the impression of this dream was still on me. Its effect was one of foreboding; but I told myself I was over the flu. But then, did this dream foretell a bout of black depression? Well, I knew what I was going to do about that, use the Siamese-twin technique, in other words, let one self give my other self a damn good swearing at.

The Siamese-twin technique proved to be of no avail. I couldn't really have been depressed. Nevertheless, I couldn't get rid of the feeling that this dream had left with me: What did it foretell? If I were going to be ill, I generally, in dreams, saw myself naked.

Three days later I said to Tom, 'I'm going to get myself outside; I want some air and there's no cure like the garden for me.'

'Go steady,' he said as he wheeled a barrow-load of dead heads and prunings to the other side of the garden.

I looked at the place where he had been working. He would take up that bunch of polyanthus next. It was a pity, for they'd go round the pond. And so, not stopping to think, I took the spade and started to dig up the clump of polyanthus. We hadn't soil in that garden, it was hard yellow clay, and this day it was wet. For the second time I pushed the spade in the ground, stuck my foot on top of the blade, pressed, and then let out a yell.

I don't remember Tom's getting me into the house, but I remember that I squealed every time he tried to move me during the next twenty-four hours. I lay for a fortnight on my back with a physiotherapist attending every other day. Following this, I could stand or lie down flat, but I couldn't sit. It was six weeks before I was up and about.

Then came the day when I again felt that I had to get outside. 'We'll go into town,' said Tom; 'it'll do you good.'

I did quite a bit of shopping in town . . . It was very cold. Two hours later, after we had returned home, I felt faint. 'Give me a glass of wine?' I said to him.

He gave me a glass of port, and I did with it what I've never done with wine before, I threw it down in one gulp.

At three o'clock I felt ill. At four o'clock I was bleeding internally.

Frantically Tom phoned the doctor. Oh, said the answering service, he couldn't have the doctor's unlisted home number; and it was no good going to the surgery, the doctor was finished.

THERE ARE DOCTORS AND DOCTORS

'My wife is bleeding internally,' said Tom.

'How old is she?' asked the man on the other end of the phone.

'Sixty-three,' said Tom.

'Well, the doctor's finished for the weekend,' said the man.

Tom bundled me into the car, and landed me on the doctor's private doorstep.

The result of the examination was the suggestion that I was either bleeding from the bladder or had acute cystitis, or my blood trouble had started up in there, or again it could be cysts on the walls of the bladder . . . I would have to see a specialist.

I bled profusely all that night and all next day, and I don't know who was in a worse state, myself or Tom. I was only vaguely aware that he never seemed to leave me.

I lay for the next four days like someone already dead. I was concerned only about two things, leaving Tom and the end of a story I had started previously about Jarrow. It was strange, I thought, and prophetic that I had to make this home town of mine my last story. I felt it imperative that I should finish it. I wanted to tell Tom the end but I hadn't the strength.

I lay until the Wednesday, and the specialist hadn't arrived. Tom phoned the doctor again. Oh, hadn't he come? Oh, they would get in touch with him.

He came that afternoon. He had heard about my trouble only that morning. He ordered me into hospital straight-away for an operation.

I would have lost all faith in doctors entirely if, a short while later, I hadn't met dear Doctor Gabb of St Leonards who was the first man to do anything about my bleeding. He introduced me to that fine surgeon Mr Ranger of the Middlesex Hospital in London who grafted skin from my hip into my right nostril and cut a wedge out of my tongue and so saved me from continual bleeding, at least from those areas and for a time.

Doctor Gabb had gone out of his way to help me while he himself was dying from cancer.

He was the only one, up to that time, who didn't put telangiectasia, the consequent anaemia, and lead poisoning, the three things I'd always suffered from, down to my imagination or temperament.

Oh, I see you've had a breakdown. What's the trouble? Temperament!!!

As one doctor added, 'Well, you know, you are a writer.'

But that dream had, in a way, foretold me there was more to it than flu, for during the bleeding I imagined I was ploughing through blood and all the while telling myself to make for the landing which, once reached, would enable me to escape death.

But at last fate has turned her face:

> I now have a panel of three,
> Who certainly see to me:
> The first my odds and bods,
> The second my nose,
> And the third
> . . . Goes where no man goes.
> So between them they
> Stretch my span.
> I can ask no more
> Of any man.

'I turned round and pressed my
back tight against the trunk,
my palms flat on the bark, and slowly
I felt the tension slipping from me . . .
it was as if the tree was saying,
"Breathe deeply."'

'I was for giving up after painting the apple, until Tom said I shouldn't attempt the strawberries, they were much too difficult ...

... He certainly knows what he's doing: I finished the strawberries and started on the cherries.'

*'That moment is all there is, and so filled with
exquisite peace that you long to spread it
over into an hour, a day, a lifetime.'* ·

THE NET

There were times when I was confined to bed for long periods and although I had to be very ill before I stopped writing or dictating my fan mail or answering innumerable telephone calls, I still, at times, felt I wanted some relief from the daily routine, and as I couldn't paint in bed I asked myself why I didn't start to draw again. So I tried; but my efforts were poor; I had lost the touch. Or was it that I was afraid of the pencil and what it had led up to thirty-five or so years before? The subconscious is ever with us.

The White Light

There arises in me at times a feeling – spiralling upwards – which eventually cork-screws out of the top of my head in a thin thread of joy. It seems to travel great distances from its source to its escape, yet it is gone even as I realise I'm experiencing it.

This feeling was very strong in me when I first experienced love. It was the one and only time it took longer than the split second in its transit through my being. This day, I was coming through the Arches from Tyne Dock on my way back to East Jarrow. How old would I have been? Eleven or twelve perhaps. There were five arches spanning the road between the dock gates and the few houses at the bottom of Simonside Bank, the place where I was born. I had passed through the first one and into the daylight, the coal-speckled, smoke-smeared daylight cut off by the high walled bank on one side and the dock wall on the other, and there, emerging from the last arch into daylight, was a boy called Hughie Aixill. He was beautiful. We had one arch each to pass through before we should meet. I kept my eyes on him while all the time feeling I couldn't bear it, I'd have to look away. And then a strange thing happened: Hughie became lost in a great white light. It spread out from him; it enveloped the great black arch and blotted out every material thing in the world: there was nothing but this great white light; and I walked into it.

When I turned round, I was beyond the fifth arch. I walked back a few steps and looked through the arches, and there he was at the far end of the last one.

What had happened? Was I going funny? Was I going daft like Delia Norton? Kate was always saying, 'Pull your stockings up. Get Charlie off your back; you're just like Delia Norton.' What had happened to me? I bowed my head. I loved Hughie Aixill.

I never saw him again until I was twenty. I was getting off the tram at the bottom of Talbot Road and there was this beautiful young man, too beautiful for a man, boarding the tram with 'a very swanky piece'.

Two things I remember: we never did speak a word to each other; and I never saw him smile; and that day when he got on the tram, his face looked as if it had never smiled.

I wondered afterwards if he was conscious of being beautiful. When I think of him now it is with gratitude for providing me with that exquisite experience.

First Love

It comes unbidden,
Shocked into light,
Like a spark
Dying while born.

It comes like
The spirit-lifting
Spurt of a lark
From nest
Hidden in grass
Tear-rimmed with dew.

But when with starved heart
We clutch
It is gone,
Dead;
Like first love
At a rough touch.

THE LODGERS
Billy Potts

Where did they sleep, the lodgers who appeared from time to time in our house during my early childhood? We had three rooms: a front room, a kitchen, and a bedroom, and yet at times there were four lodgers staying with us. When this should happen Kate and I would have to leave the dess-bed that was set in the corner of the front room and sleep on the saddle in the kitchen. This wouldn't take two abreast, and so she slept at the top of it and I at the bottom.

The saddle, by the way, was a wooden erection in the shape of a couch which was covered with a biscuit tick which didn't alleviate the hardness in the least.

There was another bed in the front room. It was set in a sort of recess between the door leading in from the small hallway and the door that led into the kitchen; and it would appear to anyone during the day that this was the only bed in this room, for the dess-bed would have been folded back behind what looked like double doors. I say four lodgers would occupy this room: it would be three and my Uncle Jack.

During this occupation by the lodgers my granda and grandma would sleep in the big brass feather-tick bed which took up more than half the space of the bedroom, the rest being taken up by a chest of drawers, a very small marble-topped wash-hand stand, with neither a basin nor a jug on it, and one of the earliest box sewing machines. You made your way into the room walking between the wash-hand stand and the sewing machine to be confronted by the small chest of drawers. You squeezed past this and there was just enough room between the bed and the wall to undress.

Where did they hang their clothes? Well, there were hooks on the back of the door and there was enough room under the bed for their cases. Where else?

I see the lodgers as all very distinct characters. One, Billy Potts, seemed to come and go. Kate would give him notice, but as soon as he heard there was a vacancy, back he would come and beg to be taken in. He had relations living above Lawsons' shop in the little street called Leam Lane where I was born. Apparently he didn't get on with them. They all drank, but he drank more than most. Yet, I never knew him to lose the use of his legs, except on one occasion. It was on Guy Fawkes Day.

It should happen that Billy was a docker, like my granda and my Uncle Jack, and he worked sometimes on the iron ore boats, sometimes on the prop boats, or he might be unloading grain. Now we always kept ducks and hens, and it was my job to go to the Jarrow store on a Saturday morning for a stone of boxings and a half stone of grain, except when Billy would be lodging with us and also helping to unload a grain boat. The hens never went short, for he would fill his trousers up to the yorks with the grain and walk past the dock polisman as steady as it was possible for him to do so carrying such an irritating cargo. Then when he entered the house Kate would put a piece of canvas on the mat and he would loosen his yorks. Yorks, by the way, are straps or pieces of string tied under the knee to hitch the trousers a little way up from the boots. In Billy's case the trousers acted as sacks for the grain.

I am sure Billy used this as a way of inveigling Kate into allowing him to stay as a lodger, for Kate had her standards. Billy was a rough, unintelligent lump of a man; moreover, he emitted body smells to which she objected.

Anyway, at this particular time Billy was the only lodger we had and he happened to be on the night shift.

Rarely, however, did he come straight home from the docks, for shovelling grain or digging out iron ore, very like lumps of clay, is a very dry job. So, he would make his way to one of the bars across from the dock gates, generally the North Eastern, as it was called, and there he would stay as long as he knew his legs were still able to carry him through the arches, up the Jarrow road and into the back door, through the kitchen and into the bedroom of 10, William Black Street. Being the only lodger he was the sole occupant of the feather bed.

As I said, it was Guy Fawkes Day and I was off school. I was always off school when the opportunity offered, and likely this day I had been kept off to go to Bob's, the pawn shop, or to do some shame-filling job for Kate, such as borrowing. Whatever it was I had earned a penny from her. This brought my secret store, which I kept in the lavatory, up to fourpence. And so I went to Cissy Affleck's little shop on the corner of Philipson Street. Here, I did something very daring, I bought the biggest firework in her shop. It was called a One O'Clock Gun. I'd heard about One O'Clock Guns and the big bang they made from the chatter of the boys who played round the shop under the lamplight at night. I understood from them there was nothing in the world to compare with the One O'clock Gun.

Now, I'd always been afraid of fireworks; Kate, too, hated fireworks and would go tooth and nail for children who threw squibs into the backyard to frighten the ducks and hens. So, I asked myself now, why on earth did I spend all that money, fourpence, on a One O'Clock Gun? I suppose I just wanted to show off. But it should be that all my friends were at school and they wouldn't be out till four o'clock, and here it was just on two o'clock and, what was more, if our Kate found me with this firework, both it and I would go up. I knew this, so I decided to hide.

We shared our backyard with a family upstairs. They must have been very patient people, the Romanuses whom I first remember occupying that house. Then the

Hoopers came, because they never objected to the hens and the ducks. But, of course, me granda kept that yard clean.

It was an ordinary backyard not more than twenty-four feet long. To the left of the door leading into the back lane were two dry lavatories; to the right of it were two coalhouses. Within four feet of the coalhouse the hen crees started and they stretched up the yard to within three feet of the bedroom window. Now, between the bedroom window and the kitchen window was a space of wall about five feet in width and standing against this was a huge rain barrel. Kate loved rain water; she had always washed herself in it and in the early days she had a good complexion. But this rain barrel left a space not more than fourteen inches wide between itself and the end of the hen cree, and nobody could get through that space, at least that's what our Kate and me granda imagined. But I'd been through it a number of times and sat on the bedroom windowsill when Kate would be at the back door yelling: 'You Katie! You Katie!' Sometimes I would sit there giggling, but more often I would be crying; and it was an easy thing to drop below the windowsill if I heard her coming into the bedroom.

So on this day I took myself and my One O'Clock Gun into my retreat and sat on the windowsill and looked in on Billy Potts lying on top of the bed. He was in his linings and he had a cap on his head, not his working cap. He always had another cap that he put on when he went to bed. He wasn't a nice sight; but worse, he wasn't a nice sound.

For the reasons I have already intimated Kate always kept the bottom of the bedroom window blocked up for about six inches. Winter and summer that window was open, and this day it was emitting these awful snores and snorts and splutters. So awful was the sight of him and the sound of him I didn't think I could stay hidden until four o'clock when my pals would come out of school and I could parade among them with me One O'Clock Gun before setting it off around the top corner. But then there were comings and goings in the yard and my emergence would give me away. Mrs Romanus had been to the corner shop and come back; one of her many children had had his ears clouted and then been flung halfway down the stairs, and now he was yelling blue murder in the yard.

I was bored; I had to do something to pass the time. I had pinched some of Kate's matches and so I knew what I would do. I would light this long piece of wick hanging out of the firework and let it sparkle for a minute, then I would nip it out; and then I would do it again, but I wouldn't let it reach the bottom, oh no.

So that's what I did.

I lit the fuse of the One O'Clock Gun, and it ignited straightaway. But instead of just sparkling it shot out myriads of lights. It petrified me. I had really never held a firework in my hand in my life, and there I was holding this big tube, and I wanted to throw it away from me – I also wanted to scream with fright – but I knew that if I threw it into the yard our Kate would see it, of course, and she would murder me. Where could I throw it? I looked through the window on to Billy Potts lying on the top of that bed. I could see some way under the bed. I knew once it got under there it would sizzle out. So, that's what I did. I pelted it through the bottom of the window and watched it roll under the bed.

When the earth exploded and I felt that the house was tumbling about my head, my scream was lost under Billy's. In a flash I remembered the missionary man talking about the cries of those suffering in hell coming up through the earth. Then as I made an attempt to squeeze through my bolthole I saw an apparition: Billy Potts was flying down the backyard; he had nothing on but his linings – his cap was gone – but he seemed to be wearing seven league boots. And then out staggered me granda and our Kate coughing and spluttering as they ran after him. And on this Mrs Romanus came tumbling down the stairs, yelling, 'Oh! Kate. Kate! Has the gas-stove blown up?'

I remember thinking, that was a silly thing to say. We had this great outsize gas-stove stuck in the corner of the kitchen between the old chest of drawers and the fire range. It had once been in some hotel. Kate had acquired it from God knows where. She would never throw anything away herself and she was very quick to collect things that were lying about. But everybody knew it was just a status symbol, because it had never been connected up.

Once again I was about to make an attempt to escape when up the yard came our Kate and me granda and between them they were almost carrying what looked like a gibbering idiot.

People had always said Billy was never the same after that. He had never been much before but what sense he had seemed to have been blown out of him. Anyway, he left the next day without our Kate telling him to go.

As for me, when I got out of me hidy-hole I dashed up the back lane and on to the fields; and there I stayed until it was dark. And our Kate never came yelling for me, but me granda did. He came through the grass, saying, 'You there? Come on out of it. Come on, come on. You there, Katie? D'you hear me? Come on out of it.'

I was frightened and I was cold, but more so I was petrified of what I would get from our Kate, but when I stood up he took my hand and he walked me over the field and past Mr Petrick's allotment. He didn't go down the back lane though, he took me down the front street, and when we came to the lamp he stopped and looked down on me. His bristly moustache was moving up and down like when he was trying to stop himself from laughing. And then his voice was nice when he said, 'You're a little bugger, aren't you? But you're a clever lass into the bargain: you've got rid of him; he's going the morrow. And that'll be the last we'll see of him.'

I always knew me granda didn't like Billy because me granda, too, had standards.

I said, 'Will our Kate murder me?' And he paused before he said, 'I don't think so, not the night . . .'

Many years later when I was working at Harton work-house and on my way home on one of my evenings off, which was every other one, there he nearly always was, standing on the dock bank among other men, some in work, most not, and he would call: 'Hello! there, Katie,' and I would answer very politely, 'Hello, Billy,' and would walk on, knowing that all the men were looking at me. But at the end of the month, when it was my pay-day, it seemed he would know and would be waiting for me, for he would step out from the men and say, 'Hello! there, Katie. How's it goin'?'

And I would stop and say, 'Oh, all right, Billy.'

Then he would say, 'You know, you get bonnier every time I see you. You're like your ma, you know, when she was young. Aye, she was a bonny lass . . . An' you're keepin' all right?'

'Yes, Billy, yes. Thank you very much.' And then my hand would go into my purse and I would give him a sixpence or a shilling – it all depended on how I had arranged my two pounds a month pay – and always he would say the same thing, 'No, lass, no. I couldn't take that,' while his hand was grasping the coin. Then he would finish, 'It'll get me a set in. Ta, lass. Ta. I'll not forget you.'

A set in meant he could go into a pub and order a gill of beer, a half-pint, and likely get talking to someone who would then stand him another. But of course you couldn't go into a pub unless you had that tanner or bob to get . . . set in.

Poor Billy Potts. I always remember him kindly, and he never held it against me that I blew him up.

The Intellectual Docker

I can't remember his name but I have a vivid picture in my mind as to what he looked like. He was about five foot three with a dour expression and he talked with a thick Scottish accent. The day he came he had two suit-cases, and the larger one was full of books. These he arrayed on top of the chest of drawers, and he must have told Kate that he didn't want any one to touch them because she straight-away warned me not to go near the man's books.

I must have been about twelve at the time and starved for reading material, and whenever I could slip into that bedroom I would pick up one of these books.

Shakespeare's plays made up the front row; the second row was of oddments, one a biography of a man named Donne, another a book of poems by a man named Browning, another by Stevenson, two by a man called Burns. But the one I was interested in was the book at the end of the Shakespeare row because in it were some poems called sonnets and then a much longer one called *Venus and Adonis*; and this one I found at first very interesting because it was all about kissing. However, I could take only the odd glimpse of this poem, and it took me some time to get to the end. I must say I found it very disappointing because the fellow goes and gets himself killed by a boar; nothing really exciting seemed to happen, and if I remember rightly she returns to her parents who were gods or something. I just couldn't get to the bottom of it all: why somebody should write all these rhymes just about kissing.

Well, it should happen that one Saturday when I was supposed to be scrubbing the lino Kate found me poring over this book. She snatched it from my hand, then said, 'I've told you! He doesn't like anybody messin' about with his books.' But she noticed what I had been reading, so she started to read it; then banged the book closed. 'Don't you ever look at that part again. It's mucky.'

Mucky? And they were just kissing.

It should happen that when the little Scot first came to lodge, unlike other lodgers, he would often stay in at nights, and when he wasn't reading he'd play cards with me. And I found him to be a kind·little fellow for when I won a game he'd give me a ha'penny. Kate accused him of letting me win. But I remember him saying, 'Oh, no, I don't; she plays straight. She's got a good head on her shoulders.'

Although he was dour and very rarely smiled, I liked the little Scot.

And then he stopped staying in at nights and our Kate kept nodding her head when she was talking to me granda on the quiet. And one day he left. He packed his books in the big case and he went down to Shields to lodge with a woman.

Now it should happen that this woman's husband went to sea for longish trips and this day his boat comes in unexpectedly and he goes home and who does he find there but the little Scot! And apparently he was very peeved, for he not only wiped the floor with him, but the walls and ceiling too, because my little friend found himself in hospital. And the sailor? Well, I think he took a one-way ticket up the line to Durham. Kate had done a lot of nodding at me granda at the time, saying, she knew what would happen and it served him right because the woman had a name.

At the time I couldn't make that last bit out. But I always remembered the little Scot, and in later years I thought of him as the 'intellectual docker'. How many dockers, I ask you, would carry with them all Shakespeare's works, the poems of John Donne, Browning, Stevenson, and his beloved Robbie Burns, and many others that were arranged on the top of that chest of drawers?

He was before his time was my little Scot. If only he had had a chance to study literature among the literary, what he might not have become. I often wondered what he thought about when he was humping pit props, shovelling grain, unloading fruit or, on the other hand, loading coal from the staithes. Did he think as Donne: 'No man is an island, entire of itself'? And did he think: 'And swear nowhere lives a woman true and fair'? Or with Burns:

> 'Or were I in the wildest waste,
> Sae black and bare, sae black and bare,
> The desert were a Paradise,
> If thou wert there, if thou were there'?

It's almost seventy years now since I last saw the little Scot, but he has lived on in my memory . . . simply because he liked books. And what books!

The 'Respectable Men'

There was, as I have said, a time when four men slept in the front room: three were lodgers called engineers, the fourth was me Uncle Jack.

These three lodgers were different because even when they went out to work they were cleanly dressed. They had come to install something on a piece of railway land opposite the sawmill a quarter of a mile down the road. I seem to remember it had to do with boilers. Another extraordinary thing about them, they didn't drink. And during their stay the house had quite a happy feeling.

I hold the picture of Kate in the washhouse. Apparently they had been in and had had their dinner and she had returned to the washhouse, and as they were leaving for work one of them stepped in, took a handful of soapy suds and threw them at her. That's all Kate needed to start a bit of fun, and so she cornered him with the hose, and there was much laughter from the other two men and begging from the culprit.

I recall I felt happy that day, as I did on a certain Saturday night when the three men and my Uncle Jack went into Shields and to a theatre. I watched them go, me Uncle Jack, too, in a good suit and a new cap. It was as if we had moved into the aristocracy. And I recall Kate's saying, 'Jack would have been a different fellow altogether if he'd had such men as those for companions and not the drinking crew from the docks.' Strange, wasn't it, that she should blame Jack for his drinking. To use her own saying, it was the kettle calling the frying pan black.

Jack must have been nineteen at the time. The following year the war broke out and he joined up straightaway. He died of his wounds two months before it ended.

I have only recently found out through the good offices of Mr Laurence Cotterell where Jack was buried, and Laurence had not only gone to the trouble of finding the cemetery but of having a photograph of the gravestone taken, and, also at my request, a laurel wreath put on it: To my Uncle Jack. From Katie.

Snatches of the day the telegram came to say that he had died of his wounds come back to me. I took it from the boy at the front door and read it to me granda, and he cried and said, 'I've been expecting it. I told him he should never take that stripe.' And when Kate came back from the Jarrow store, from where she had got a club and was buying bed linen to prepare a comfortable bed for the wounded hero, she too cried, then said to me, 'It's God's will, because if he had come back there would have been no home for either of us here.'

And I can understand that now because he had wanted her when he was a young fellow, but now that he was a seasoned man things would have been impossible for her.

I lay in the dess-bed that night and prayed for his soul. I knew he would be in Purgatory because of his sins, for not only did he drink and want to fight, but he wouldn't get up in the morning to go to work, and Kate had to yell at him and a row would ensue. He was bound to be in Purgatory. But prayers could get people out of Purgatory, and so every night I prayed for me Uncle Jack to be released from that torment, and gradually, gradually, I saw him rising up, until one night there he was, standing behind great iron gates, and he said, 'Hello, Katie.' And I said, 'Hello, Uncle Jack.' But I became troubled. What was I to do with him? Where would he go when I let him through those gates? I didn't know. So, being the coward I was, I didn't wait to find out but left him there, and I didn't pray for him any more.

But every now and then over the long years I have thought of Jack and of how, if he'd had the chance to have been brought up away from his father's pattern, drink and the docks, he would, as Kate had said, have been different, because he was an attractive looking man in a dark gypsy-ish way, and I look kindly back on him because he was kind to me. In fact, I think, as me granda did so he, too, loved me. But now he's lying quietly in France all because he woke up one morning in the barracks in Shields very surprised to find that he was in the Army. He and his pal had enlisted the previous night in the throes of drunken enthusiasm, so drunk that he could never remember signing his name.

And now, thanks to Laurence, I know where he lies. I won't bother praying for him again for he is at peace and has been for a long time. Wherever he is I hope he knows, 'Our Katie', as he called me, still thinks of him, thinks of the night he tasted a different way of life when in a good suit he went to a theatre with three respectable lodgers.

My Brothers, 1916

You tell me, speak well of all men;
You are all brothers.
But my brothers have lain down
In foreign fields to rest
With an ease of which they are not aware,
Or that they have left
Their gifted youth
Sponsor to manhood they will never know,
Because men, bearded and gray,
Braids on caps and pips on shoulders,
Wanted to play a game of war,
On paper, for their part,
With pins in maps.
Seated at long tables, in leather chairs,
They sent their orders to advance
To youths
To prove themselves in the dance
Of bullets and bayonets going through bellies,
For is there not Glory in dying?
Do they not share their limbs
With their mates'?
Now they are all brothers under the sod.
                    Oh brother!
                    Oh God!

The Soldier, 1916

Sand and sea
Separate me
From you;
Rock, mountain and snow
Freeze my memory,
Rain, wind and sleet
March with me,
Mud clogs my feet;
Orders bellow in my head;
The ground my bed,
The sky my quilt
Stitched by stars.
In this mêlée
You should be far away from me
O'er land and sea
And mountain range,
From battles and blood;
Yet deep inside my being
Where no paths lead
You are fast in times gone
And all our lives ahead,
So should I die
You will be with me:
We shall not be dead.

GETTING TO SLEEP

There are some nights when I'm still talking into my tape recorder at half-past eleven. These are the times when my mind is deep in the story, when all the characters are around me: I'm expressing their thoughts, jumping from one to another, my voice emitting words used in ordinary conversation or those erupting in temper or soft in sympathy; or perhaps raking in the depths of a mind for the hidden reasons for actions and reactions to events that may not be every day occurrences.

Well, imagine what my mind is like after going through that gamut, perhaps for three or four hours previously, and Tom popping in every now and again saying, 'Come on now! Aren't you going to finish?' and I answering, 'I must get this down while it's hot.'

And while it's hot my mind gets practically to boiling point, and it's often still simmering away when Tom turns the light out and says finally, 'Now stop thinking, and get to sleep,' to which I invariably reply, 'You get to sleep; you need it more than I; I'm lying flat most of the day.'

Then the retort: 'I'm not going to sleep until you do.'

Three minutes later he's puffing away gently, and there I am, in a whirlpool full of grasshopping thoughts, all jumping over each other as if trying to get out. So what do I do? I tell myself to relax.

Huh! The times I've said that during my life: relax.

It is many years now since I taught myself how to get out of the whirlpool and knock my grasshopping thoughts on the head. And it works if I follow my 'instructions' implicitly. But that's the snag, to get your mind to turn on itself; and the only way I found I could achieve this was by talking to every part of my body and treating each section as if it had a separate life of its own.

Before starting on this process, however, I resort to a special place. Mine is a kind of beach: an endless sea ahead, an endless expanse of beach on either side; but behind, there is a high thicket of greenery that acts as a barricade against the world. And sometimes on this beach is an animal to whom I talk. But I will come to that later.

As now, there I am lying on this warm *sand*, and I start with my left foot and I tell it, it is very tired and it must let go and drop deep into the sand. And this it does. Then I move from the ankle up to the calf and have another little natter. The knee gets quite a bit of attention. Following this, I pause to find out if the limb has obeyed my orders. More often than not it has. I repeat this process with the right leg; then with the left thigh, and the right thigh.

Now I come to the stomach. When one is tense the intestines seem generally knotted up, all twenty-five feet of them. So I speak firmly to them, having a little word with each organ around them.

Now I come to the lungs. Take it easy, I tell them, take it slowly: take longer to breathe out than to breathe in; let it feel as though the air is going right down to the stomach. That's better.

There are times when I never get to my arms, my shoulders or my head, and wake up the next morning, and conclude that the rest must have got the message and could no longer be bothered to listen to my jabbering.

The truth is that it doesn't always work: sometimes I do reach the top of my head and have to start at the toes again. But by this time the mechanism is definitely slowing down and the second time around invites sleep and I'm off; perhaps by this time it's two o'clock in the morning.

As the years went on and I began to suffer the results of my physical labours, which included not only ordinary housework but also outside manual labour, such as the sawing down of trees, sawing them up, dragging great branches through woodland, humping turfs, and, at one time single-handed, the making of concrete paths and quite a large fish pond. Looking back to that period, I wonder how on earth I fitted that in between the running of a laundry and also that of a guest house. But nevertheless, I did, and I think the pond is still in evidence in the garden of my first house in Hastings.

Well, as I said, the accumulation of my labours resulted in muscular pains that at times made sleep impossible, and as I am very much averse to taking drugs of any kind, I needed help of some form, so I brought on to my restful island a pair of invisible hands. There was no body at all to these hands, but when I wasn't up to prattling to my ailments I would conjure up these hands and they would massage my painful limbs. They would have the same effect as my voice, and eventually I would sink deep into the mattress and sleep would thankfully overtake me.

Now all this is mind over matter and the using of one's imagination, and no matter what anyone thinks to the contrary, little or much, it works. As does the talking to an animal.

I think I have already mentioned the book *Feeling Fine* by Dr Art Ulene. This man is an American doctor and broadcaster, and his book covers a course of twenty-one consecutive daily lessons designed to reach harmony and peace within oneself. I read it and practised his suggestions for a time. What struck me forcibly was his advocating talking to animals. Choose an animal, make it a confidante and talk to it, he said. Instead of talking to thin air you have this friend, this animal, be it a dog, cat, a giraffe, lion, tiger, what you fancy. He himself, his wife and his family, each had his animal. Believe it or not I chose a hippopotamus. Yes, yes, a hippopotamus; perhaps because he was an ugly animal, rather unloved, and therefore he always seemed to me to be lonely. Well, one night I was lying on my beach when, there suddenly I found him lying on the sand beside me; and I talked to him for I knew him to be but the representation of my inner spirit, that small still voice of my conscience, and I am not being blasphemous when I say an animal placed in this position could be God's messenger, for I do believe He uses all kinds of people, places and things to make Himself plain.

After my introduction to Hippo I wrote an article entitled: 'God Is A Hippopotamus'. I never published it because I knew that it would bring such a storm of letters, and as I am absolutely inundated with letters from all kinds of kind people who want to give me their God and who promise me, if I believe as they do, I shall know peace of mind and spirit to such an extent that I couldn't imagine possible. Over the past years I have written back to these dear people and told them that I have already gained peace of mind and spirit to such an extent that I never imagined possible, and without resorting to any particular denomination.

How has it come about? Perhaps lying on that beach talking to my body, perhaps talking to Hippo, perhaps because I've learned to understand fear for fear has been my dire opponent and I know it can never be overcome by fearing it. Fear is fear's comrade: you fear it and it will grow in strength; swear at it, send it to hell, whatever, but stand up to it.

Brave words! All right, all right. I, too, have said these derisive words to myself countless times.

There are all kinds of fears. What about a fear that makes you sick because you want to do something wrong? You want to hurt someone. This is one of the worst. Well, if you feel sick with the fear of hurting someone, that battle is already half won because you know in yourself you'll never do it. Nevertheless, that is the time you should go to your own particular beach, or room, or whatever place you choose to be by yourself in your mind, and put all your cards on the table, and there, with your dog, your cat, your horse, or your hippopotamus, work it out, talk it out with them. You'll get an answer. *Yes, you will*, but more likely than not it may not be the answer you want. You'll find you've got to do something entirely different from what you imagined you should do. But you can bet your life the answer that your animal friend will give you will be the right one because your animal friend is merely the representation of that intangible something, that omnipresent, omniscient mystery that no-one of us will ever be able to solve, yet to which we are attached through the spirit of it.

Strange Fears

The long twilight seeps into the night,
And from its darkening face
Heaven's eyes peer
And tell the moon the path is clear
For its crescent ride
And so my fancy paints
The mystery
To hide the fear
Of this great eternal void.
The only comfort is to think
That within it heaven lies,
And, further comfort still, I find
That I can encompass it all within my mind.

Sleeplessness

What is the night made for?
Why take away the sun
If not to beckon sleep?
I ask such questions
Of the myriad lights
That star my eyes;
And if this sleep I crave meant death
Would I long for it
As now with each nerve-racked breath?
The electric blanket,
The mattress, double sprung,
Do nothing to entice flight into phantasy.
'Twould seem the gift of sleep
Cannot be wooed;
The gods alone select those
On whom it be bestowed.

SPIRITUAL HEALING

When I returned to Hastings in 1945, I was in a very bad way, both mentally and physically. Added to this, I straightaway developed mastitis; this, after banging into my breast the long handles of a pair of tree shears: they were meant to snap off a branch; instead, they levelled me to the ground.

But the most painful development at that time was in my cheek, just underneath the eye. It had nothing to do with the bleeding.

Catarrh, said my doctor.

On my fifth visit he sighed and said, 'Oh, let's have a look.'

He looked; then exclaimed, 'Good gracious! You've got a bloody great antrum. That'll have to be seen to . . . Operation.'

It should happen that my greengrocer hadn't called for two weeks. Where had he been? On holiday?

Holiday! no; in hospital, he said, and if he had known as much as he knew then the antrum would have still been in his nose . . . it was hell!

It should happen that a friend of mine had for some time been trying to get me to 'The House of Healing' in Hastings. This house was run by a small staff of spiritual healers and spiritualists. And so, such being my condition and need of help, I found myself there, one night, sitting in on a seance, and in such a state of nerves that even the fear which consumed me each day in the breakdown paled

155

under it. I sat there listening to people 'getting messages' from the little woman at the top of the table who was in a sort of trance. She kept pausing and saying, 'I am getting interruptions here. There is someone trying to find out who has lost a friend by his own hand. He has a message for this person.'

She asked round the table, with no effect.

She was in the middle of giving another message when, her finger pointed straight at me, she cried, 'He's standing behind you! and he says you are not to worry any more about him; it was done on the spur of the moment. His name is . . . is John, and he is at peace now.'

Oh John! I almost shouted.

John had been a friend of mine who had got into money difficulties and had shot himself two years previously. His going had worried me for I had been near to following his example.

The woman then startled me even further by saying, 'There is someone else with him, and he's very old. He says you are to return to your own way of working, to how your heart dictates. He says, do you understand?'

Did I understand? Oh yes, I understood.

For almost a year I had been studying grammar because Tom thought I should, and so I was writing grammatically, and so correctly that my characters had been mere puppets of the English language.

I couldn't get away quick enough and go to the Grammar School where Tom was taking his scout troop, and tell him what had happened. Strangely, he showed no surprise, but agreed that, yes, it would be better if I returned to my own way of writing . . .

Now this happened just before my chat with the greengrocer; so it wasn't surprising that I should find myself one night lying on a table, and the little woman – the same one who had taken the seance – was pressing my face and talking, talking, talking.

My friend had told me that these people never hurt you when giving treatment.

Later, I stood waiting for the bus while crying my eyes out with pain.

After alighting from the bus I had about a mile to walk to my home. I arrived about 9.30. This was on the Friday night.

On Monday morning, I was in the bathroom washing my face. I bent over and sluiced it; and in the process of doing so, I stopped. I hadn't been able to do that for over a year. I felt my face, while staring into the mirror. I could feel no pain anywhere. Then it dawned upon me that I hadn't felt anything since I had left the bus on the Friday night; in fact, I hadn't given it further thought. The time between had seemed blank.

This, my first experience of spiritual healing, happened forty-one years ago. The antrum trouble has never returned.

A year or two later I tried to get in touch again with this same woman, but was told she had gone back to Wales. I have often thought of that little woman.

How then did I come to write to Harry Edwards, the Healer? I'm not quite sure. I think perhaps I had come across his monthly magazine. How long I'd been writing to him up till 1952, I don't know either; I can only remember I'd had three operations on the womb, and I was in the throes of a bad menopause when I heard from my aunt in the North that my mother was very ill and that I should go and see to her. She would have to be looked after.

This fear that I should one day have to bring her back again into my life had been a constant nightmare. I could see another breakdown looming up. I talked it over with Tom. He said I must bring her home; if not, it would be on my mind for the rest of my life.

I understood she had grown to an enormous size with dropsy and the drink. So how was I to get her from South Shields to Hastings?

I wrote to Harry Edwards giving him details and asking for help and strength to carry out what appeared to me to be the final life-destroying plan. He answered, you will be helped.

I found my mother in an awful state, but as dominant as ever. She was able to walk only a step or two.

Well, I can't explain it, but what followed was on oiled wheels: A St John's ambulance cheerfully took us to Newcastle station, where a night berth had been booked. There, porters hoisted my mother up on the luggage lift, then eased her sideways into the carriage and onto the bed, where she slept until six o'clock the next morning. Before seven o'clock another ambulance arrived to take us across London to Charing Cross station. The men settled us in the train.

At Hastings we were met by a further ambulance, and so to The Hurst. Her northern doctor had said, she would bother me for only two weeks at the most, and this prognosis was confirmed by the Hastings doctor.

Well, in my autobiography I explain how for years I'd wanted her dead, but now I knew she must not die until we both found ourselves.

I kept her alive for three years. It was a test, but thank God I passed it, and with the help of Harry Edwards, for he became my spiritual stay during that period. He was the understanding doctor I'd never had, until, as I've said, I met Doctor Gabb of St Leonards.

Harry Edwards performed no miracle for me, but, strangely, whenever I received a letter back from him in answer to a cry for help, I seemed to gain the strength to carry on, even while not believing in his theory that the help did not come actually from him, but that he was merely a channel for doctors working through spirit.

Perhaps it was the very name, doctors, that caused my scepticism.

It was in 1954 that so much was happening in my literary career, and so much within my physical frame.

The Rank Organisation had taken *A Grand Man* to make a film under the title *Jacqueline*. They asked me to go to Ireland and set the scene and write the first script.

I was waiting to go into hospital to have a hysterectomy; and I was bleeding severely from all points west; but to be asked by a film company to go to Ireland and set the scene, and do the script for my own book, well! I would have made the attempt, I think, had it been from my coffin.

When I came back I felt desperately ill and mentally worried. To have a hysterectomy was, I understood then, to be finished as a woman. I was forty-eight years old, Tom was six years younger. We were both still very much in love. I had failed in giving him a family, and now this.

I wrote to Harry Edwards telling him of my state of mind.

Two days later I received a letter from the hospital saying, I was to be there in five days time. This was a Friday.

On the Sunday I was lying on the couch in the drawing-room watching Tom mow the lawn. The sun was shining. My mother was dozing.

Did I hear the voice? Or did I feel the voice as an urge? Whatever . . . something said to me, '*Get up and go into the garden and put your hands into the earth.*'

I was in my nightie. I slowly rose from the couch and walked out and into the garden and knelt down on the rough cement path and began to weed the flower border. The next minute Tom was by my side exclaiming, 'Get up! Get up! What are you doing?'

'I'm putting my hands into the earth,' I said, 'Please, Please, leave me alone.'

My mother's face appeared and her expression said, another breakdown. She can't blame me for this.

Tom brought me a cushion to kneel on. I stayed there for an hour. The next day, Monday, I did the same.

It was Tuesday when I received a reply from Mr Edwards saying, among other things, 'Don't worry, you are being helped.' I said to Tom, 'Phone the hospital and say I won't be coming.'

The bleeding from inside had stopped . . . I still have my ovaries.

I think what Mr Edwards taught me, too, was to rely on that inner voice that is always waiting to be heard. He seemed to lead me to books that were of invaluable help, such as Ralph Waldo Trine's *In Tune With The Infinite*. This is a remarkable book, and to this day I refer to it as one would to a Bible. Published in 1897, it meets the mental and spiritual needs of today.

But to return to Harry Edwards. I mentioned his name to someone the other day, and the response was, 'Who is he?'

I could imagine someone saying, 'Who's Catherine Cookson?' but not, 'Who's Harry Edwards?' or 'Who was Harry Edwards?' not after he was known to have given healing treatment to members of the British and other royal families, to peers and peeresses, to cabinet ministers, judges, bishops, and an archbishop, not counting all the celebrities of stage and screen and then the ordinary people who have flocked to him in thousands. I met him only once. He was doing a demonstration in the theatre on the Hastings Pier. I was one of hundreds watching him straighten limbs. People using walking sticks would be helped up onto the stage, then walk down unaided. Whether by manipulation or by some other means, this tubby and ordinary looking man was actually enabling people to walk again.

I recall, I stood in an apparently endless line and waited my turn to state my need, and to feel the touch of his hand.

Later, thinking about the happening on that Sunday afternoon, I again discarded the spirit doctors. What was coming through that man, I felt, was straight from the power, God, if you like. As I've said, he performed no miracles for me, but what he seemingly did was to open doors out of which came unexpected help. This was very much apparent in my mother's case, even after I had got her home. I'd had indifferent treatment from doctors but with this man I only had to lift the phone and help or advice was immediately forthcoming, and this was finally dem-

'Here would I lie
For ever
If the sun remained still . . .'

'My next urge in the painting line was for skies,
sunrises and sunsets . . .

. . . When confined to my room
I would try to catch the essence of them
from my bedroom windows.'

'Altogether, I think I attended the
Hereford Art School half a dozen times,
and this still life was the third attempt
at water colour.
I'm not ashamed of that one.'

onstrated when my mother was helped to die a painless death.

Godfrey Winn said of Harry Edwards: 'I look upon this man as one of the greatest men in the world', and there are thousands of others who think the same of the young lad who at fourteen years of age was apprentice compositor in a printing firm, only to find he didn't much care for printing. And so, early in 1914 he joined the Royal Sussex Regiment and in 1915 found himself in India. Eventually he found himself in the Middle East and one day being promoted on the field from corporal to a commission in the Royal Engineers.

He knew nothing about engineering, but was given charge of a labour force made up of scores of wild nomadic Arabs and was ordered to lay a railway track linking sections between Baghdad and Mosul.

His life in this region from then until he returned to England in 1923, after having become a sort of uncrowned king, would make an adventure book in itself. He was known as Hakim for quite unwittingly he was looked upon as a healer; and this is mentioned briefly in his own book. His medical supplies were bandages, iodine and castor oil. At times, he was amazed how quickly the castor oil cured unusual things!

He felt very squeamish at the sight of wounds and considered it the bravest act he ever performed when a Mohammedan priest brought his son to him for surgery. The boy had an abscess under a great welt of bony skin on the sole of his foot. When, trembling, Harry Edwards took a razor blade and cut deep through the skin and cleaned the abscess and the boy remained calm and felt no pain whatever, he felt shaken in more ways than one. The boy's gratitude was so great he offered to be his servant for life.

His fame spread. A sheik with a mounted escort brought his mother, a very old wizened dame, to see him. She was in great pain. He wanted her cured! Edwards was in a quandary. If he didn't do something, the sheik could make trouble, big trouble. He had nothing but castor oil to give her. So he had to think of something. His interpreter had told him how serious it was. He went into his tent, made four pills out of some pink carbolic toothpaste (army issue); then, handing these to the sheik, told him to give his mother one each morning.

Some days later, he thought it was his last day when a cavalcade of armed horsemen galloped up to the camp, firing their rifles. His interpreter fled.

The sheik got down from his horse; he was laughing. His mother was quite well: here was a bag of gold!

No, thank you.

Well, what would Hakim like? He would bring some carpets.

No, thank you. But he saw that the sheik was displeased.

'Oh well,' he said; he was so glad to know that his mother was well and he'd be happy to have a few eggs for his breakfast, if that was possible.

The sheik returned with his men that same afternoon carrying baskets holding 300 eggs!

Before Harry Edwards left Persia he had under his control no less than 250,000 men, women and children. Whenever he could he had brought food to the starving and justice to the oppressed, and all the while he had brought comfort and healing to the sick.

I could go on writing about the man, but then I would simply be reiterating what Mr Ramus Branch has written about him. He and his wife Joan, both healers, worked with Harry Edwards for some years before he died, and after his death they took over the Healing Sanctuary and carried on his work. Mr Branch gives us a clear portrait of the whole man in his book, *Harry Edwards: The Life and Study of a Great Healer*.

As I am an agnostic to Christianity so I am to Spiritualism; yet can I say I am an agnostic to what is called Spiritual Healing?

The Question

Where do I go from here?
Don't tell me
Nothingness,
Into which no thought of mine
Will flow:
Dead, dead, deaded flesh
Meshed into mushed wood
And soil,
Rotten, spoiled,
Pressed down,
Food for geologists
In future mist-filled time.

Or still into nothingness
Burned,
While slow
Music drawn curtains
Bring flowing tears
Of the mourners
And fears
Of their turn.

Ashes spread around a rose
Cannot think
As they sink
Into the sod.
There must be something more,
There must;
If only for comfort now
I'll believe in God.

Why Are We Born?

The greatest mystery of life is death.
The greatest fear of life is death.
The greatest sorrow in life is death.
The greatest probe in life is for death.

Why then are we born?
Suckling the breast,
Crawling to walk,
Chattering to talk,
Opening ears to take in others' lives:
Habits from eons past;
Then galloping through the false
Values of youth,
Searching for truth,
And love
Beyond cohabiting.
Giving birth,
Giving birth,
Giving birth
Becomes weary,
While the childless life
Is tear filled and dreary.
Disharmony and parting rend the years.

Now the ungodly
Grab the straw
And join their fears
To the believers
Who tremble against
The coming last breath
That leads to death.

Again, why are we born
If not to learn how to die?

WHO PRAYS NOW?

I would have said I have never prayed since I gave up organised religion. Then rather late in life I learned that prayer, after all, is just the compilation of thoughts; and, what was more, that which I had termed 'just thought' was the most powerful weapon known to the human race, for without its use nothing is possible.

It was during the dark days of my life when I was crying out for the two wonders of the world, peace of mind and the joy of living, that one day out of the blue I added the words 'and the power to make other people happy'.

Now during that particular period I couldn't understand why I should even for a moment think about making people happy, for all my life I had bothered about people, certain people, and what had it brought me? A breakdown: a tormented mind, a brain riddled with fear. So why concern myself about other people being happy? I must be barmy. For once in my life, I wanted to be able to say, 'I'm all right, Jack.'

Years passed, during which time I worked never less than fourteen hours a day, and gradually, gradually my fears had subsided. They erupted at intervals, but when they did so I was able, more or less, to say to them, 'You are nothing but the figments of twisted imagination, coupled with superstition, threaded together with retaliation born of the past experiences. I can manage you.'

But even so, after all those long, laborious years I still

hadn't experienced that nirvana derived from peace of mind and the joy of living. As for making people happy, well it seemed ridiculous that each night, just before dropping off to sleep, I would add this request to my two main desires and then suggest them to my subconscious.

Why did I keep it up? Why?

Then one morning I was given the answer.

Over the years my fan mail has been growing and growing, and nearly all the letters I receive tell in some part of them how the writer enjoys my books. On this particular morning I had opened the seventh letter before it struck me that each one had begun with the same line, 'Dear Mrs Cookson, I am writing to thank you for the pleasure and happiness your books have given me.' Four of them went on to say that they had even been of more help to them than anything else in their lives. And this applied especially to my autobiography.

But it was the first line that hit me. Here were seven people, four from England, one from Wales, one from America, and one from Australia, all saying the same thing, that I had, in some way, brought them happiness; and it came to me like a revelation that for years now I had been asking for peace of mind and the joy of living and that I had been receiving a good share of the former through being given the power to write, and this in its turn had apparently made a number of people happy.

Because of my sales I knew that my writing must be of interest to a great many people, and their letters had expressed to me their pleasure over the years, yet it wasn't until that moment when these seven letters began with the same sentence that I realized it was because of my third desire that I had been given a good measure of my first request.

The longer I live the more I realise that our lives, to a great extent, are the outcome of what we pray for, or in other words, of what we continuously and persistently think.

As I Would Have It

Our Father
Who is as a power
Through all the universe,
I would like to revere You,
And be happy in doing so.
We will take it at the start
That goodness alone
Comes from You and no evil;
We want from You the power
To earn our living
In a way that will bring us contentment,
And the power to resist harming human or
*   animal,*
And the power to forgive ourselves our
*   misdeeds,*
And the power to resist anything
That our deep heart tells us is wrong,
And the power to direct our mind
To the realization that we are part of a great
*   mystery*
That will one day be made clear to us,
And hope that this will help us to come
Near to You and say,
In all humility,
Thy will be done.

Gods

He was born a Catholic,
A Protestant,
A Nonconformist,
A Buddhist,
How stupid is phraseology
When speaking of theology.

He was born a Negro,
A Chinaman,
A Russian,
An Israelite.
Black, brown, white or yellow,
His genes set the test
And to heat left the rest,
But nowhere in his seed
Was God in this deed.

Since, first, man beheld the sky
And whimpered, What is there?
Did a being
Bigger than the begetter
Rise in his mind
And, towering tall,
Filling life with fear
To the rim,
Obliterate the truth
That God the Creator
Is in himself . . . him?

MUSIC

Yesterday when walking in the wood I was reminded of a poem I wrote and set to music. It was while I was waiting for Tom to be discharged from the RAF. I was alone in The Hurst, fifteen rooms of emptiness; I was still in the breakdown but my mind was alert, over alert, and during that period I composed a number of tunes and gave them lyrics. This particular one was set off by watching the falling leaves. I was thinking of children, at the time . . . the children I had lost.

> Come fly out of doors and see the rain,
> Rain that won't come for a year again,
> Golden rain brittle and brown
> Singing as it floats waverly down.
> Come let joy sing in your veins
> For only once a year it rains
> Leaves of autumn, yet promise of spring.
> Come fly out of doors
> And let your heart sing.

A couple of years ago my cousin, Sarah, was staying with me. One day she was playing the piano, and something about the tune caught my attention. 'What was that?' I asked her.

She laughed at me but didn't answer; then seeing I was waiting she stopped playing and said, 'Don't you know?'

'I wouldn't have asked you if I did.'

'Well, you composed it,' she said.

And then I remembered I had written a poem called, 'Let the beauty linger in my soul' – I was to use this in my first novel some years later and I remembered how I had set it to music.

Electric shock treatment had in my case the power to make me forget things I wanted to remember and to remember things I would rather have forgotten.

The poem went as follows:

Solace

Let the beauty linger in my soul
Of a rose just bursting into bloom,
Of a bird in flight,
Of the moon, new born into the night,
Reflecting on a sea of gentle ripples.

Let the beauty linger in my soul
Of a winter morn draped in patterned frost,
Of air like wine,
Of sunlit snow on limbs of trees,
Of black-brown trunks bare to the winds that
    sweep the woods,
Of drifts of crisp brown leaves,
Swept, now here, now there, with the breeze.

Let the beauty linger in my soul
Of firelight in a darkened room,
Of kindly words,
Of lovers' laughter coming through the night,
Until, at last, I know no greater peace or ease
Than to remember these.

This sounds a little trite to me now, but at that particular time I longed to be touched by beauty, of any kind, and oh how I longed for 'peace or ease' of mind.

When I look back over the years I'm amazed how I ever came through that period; that long period of time when every hour of every day was filled with the battle against fear.

With regard to music I know what I like. It must have a tune to it. I like some modern songs yet I can't stand pop, but anything by Jim Reeves or Roger Whittaker has the power to soothe my nerves.

I like Mozart, Liszt and Chopin. But I shy away from the heavy classical, although there are certain pieces by Beethoven that I like.

Yet, some time ago I realised I was missing something by not understanding classical music. I put it down to the fact that I didn't listen, really listen. I came to the conclusion that to understand music it was no good having it as a background, you had to sit down and in a way read it through your ears, and this I endeavoured to do. I started by picking out the different instruments and trying to follow the theme they were taking.

This was all right for about five to ten minutes and then an odd thing would happen. I would still be listening but I would be interpreting the music to my own way of thinking, one particular part would represent the sea, another a woodland scene, another sorrow, anger, joy, and before I knew where I was they were forming a story in my mind.

Time and again I tried to separate my way of thinking from what I was hearing but it was no use. I couldn't, I found, listen to music without using it in a way that my mind was trained to work, so every time I listen to music now, pleasant music, it creates scenes in my mind, it intensifies passion or compassion, love or hate. I get up in the middle of a piece of music and start writing furiously.

I've left it too late to understand music, but not too late for me to use it.

DEATH

Death is the only thing we can be sure of attaining on our own. It's a very personal thing, death. Someone once said to me she was afraid of dying alone, but when you come to think about it you can't die any other way – you go out on your own.

At one time I was petrified at the thought of dying, and not a little peeved that all these great thoughts of mine would be extinguished. This was, of course, in my early days before I was forced to face up to my ignorance. But now I can hardly believe that I have lost my fear of my final departure and look upon it almost as an adventure; supposing there *is something* there; if not, then I'll feel nothing, it'll just be like a long dreamless sleep.

I think I am able to look at death this way because I've had a good span, during which I have experienced nearly all human emotions; but if I were young what would my idea of it be then? Oh, vastly different I suppose, especially if I were made aware that I hadn't long to live. Death is unfair to the young; it's unfair to their parents, and to all those who love them.

A friend of mine recently lost a daughter just turned twenty. She was so full of life, she loved life, she wanted to live, and she had so much to live for, so much talent to work out; and then she died, a slow lingering death in a London hospital. She died on a machine that kept her breathing, and only that, for she had lost the use of all her limbs and her speech and her sight.

173

DEATH

One thing that struck me was that her dying brought good out of many people. Yet I asked the question: Couldn't the good in them have been made evident through a less traumatic way?

Oh God spare youth
To see this life,
To experience the love, the joy,
The anguish, the wonder, the strife;
Don't deprive them of summer
While in their spring,
Give them the chance
To let their minds soar,
To let their hands clutch the mountain tops,
Their bodies to dive deep from the rock;
Don't cut short their time
On the ancient clock of destiny;
Keep from their marrow
Disease that is due to age;
Don't take their breath
While yet they fear death;
Give them a span in which to know courage
Is the friend of pain;
Give them the time to love, be a wife
And create themselves again;
But if You must take them,
Do it before they smell
The scent of life.

The Rejected Gift

I long to cry: slow tears or fast
Flowing down my face, licking the salt as they
*   pass,*
Mounting on my chin,
Then falling to my chest,
Washing out the strain
And bringing me to rest.

Oh, the relief of tears,
The joy in their flowing.

The unrecognised gift of God
The Great Unknown
Whom we bless for happiness and laughter
All down the years
And pray the we and ours be spared tears.

If I cry I bleed.
Why doesn't God understand my need?

SUCCESS

1960s

∽

Success – I suppose it's what most people crave for. They work and slave and tear their innards out for it. And in the end – for what?

Only those who have known success know the penalty that it brings. Often the payment for it is an early death – or at least a heart attack, brought about by the doubling of demands on them.

It's no use telling people that the main thing success has done for you has been to make you wiser to the extent that you realise the ephemerality of it, and the fact that in a very short time you will be dead and who will remember you, literally speaking? Oh, I know I've a great following now, but so had so many writers, great writers, men and women much better at their job than I am, and do you hear their names mentioned? No; a new generation comes up and favours a new cult, a new style.

I've had so many different reactions to my success. I've had praise from those I look up to and admire. I've been slapped on the back and had my ego expanded by others; then there are those who have said, on a laugh, 'Clever bugger, aren't you?' and to that has been added more than once, 'Why, if I had the time I could write your kind of stuff; you're not the only one who's had it hard, you know . . . Now take me mother.' Or, 'Now I've got a story, and don't mind me saying this, but it's as good as any of yours I've read. No offence meant mind, but it

176

wants putting together, with grammar an' that. How about it?'

But one gets over these types; the ones that get under one's skin are those that never open their mouths.

As I have indicated, success can do odd things to us, and it *can* make you wish you hadn't known it. This was brought home to me one day when I met a man whom I had known as a boy, and his reactions to his success saddened me.

So I put down what he said in my usual short lines, and I headed it:

My First Pair of Boots

I was nine when I got me first pair of boots,
New ones I mean, that fitted:
Bulbous toes and hobnailed soles
And leather laces broad
And strong as whipcord
You had to suck the end bits
To get them through the eyelets.

I didn't kick a can that day
Or walk in the clarty gutters,
I never chucked a brick
Or thought of playing the nick
But got to school so quick
You'd've thought I'd been kicked in the
*   backside by me mother.*
Best part of the day I kept one foot stuck in
*   the aisle*
So Miss Platt could see me boot,
But all she did was step over it and remain
*   mute,*

She didn't even go for Mulligan when he said
'Are ya ganna tyek 'em off when ya gan
*   t'bed?'*
When the bell rang I was the last to leave.
It was then Miss Platt touched my sleeve
And looking down at me boots she said,
'They're grand boots, whoppers, keep them
*   clean, Steve.'*

I now have twenty pairs on a rack
All for different occasions to match the clothes
*   on me back,*
But where's the pride and where's the joy
Of that first pair of hobnailed boots
I had when a boy?

Immortality

All, all forgotten:
Hadrian, Shakespeare, Churchill
Fade under the sun like frosted rime.
Their words and their works remain,
But the men?
Just names on a page,
Buried cities
Of an age
The mind can't grasp.
All that remains
A shell
That crumbles to the touch.
Words only convey an image,
Insubstantial wisps of thought
That go for nought.
Everlasting fame is a fancy
In the heart of man,
At best to be remembered
In love
For the length of a lifetime.

THE PRAYER OF MARY ELLEN SPIER

All my writings as Catherine Cookson deal with life, and some of it can be pretty grim, and so I attempt to lighten it here and there with flashes of humour brought over through a particular character.

In *Fenwick Houses*, which is the story of a beautiful young woman who is fated to bring unhappiness on herself, I lighten one part which deals with a birthday party where the heroine's brother takes the mickey out of a neighbour who is a maiden lady.

It is a pre-war story and in those days laughter could be evoked by simple things, such as the following:

The Prayer of Mary Ellen Spier

O Lord, she said, look after me
And don't make me like the likes of she
Who, next door, in dark sin abounds,
A lip-stick, rouge and film hound.

O Lord, I beg, look after me
Who only ever imbibes tea;
Not like others with drops of gin,
Which is the stimulant of sin.

THE PRAYER OF MARY ELLEN SPIER

O Lord, I beg, take care of me
From all those men who go to sea;
Shield me, I pray, from their winks,
And don't blame me, Lord, for what I thinks.

And from those men who swarm the air,
Fair bait I am for them up there.
If I am not to become a flyer
Work overtime, Lord, on . . .
        Mary Ellen Spier.

From actors, Lord, protect me proper,
Or else I'll surely come a cropper;
Keep my dreams all dull and void,
And lock the door, Lord, on . . . Charles
        Boyd.

Let me not mix, Lord, I pray,
With poets and writers of the day;
Keep my hands from their craft,
And stop me, Lord, from going daft.

And when I die, oh Lord, remember
My life has been one grey December;
I ain't never had men, wine or beer,
And, O Lord, ain't I bored down here!

CHILDREN FROM AFAR

Sister Catherine Marie in her convent in California teaches Mexican Indian children, and to my amazement I learned that over the years they have read my books. And so, when they knew I was ill, they sent me a big scroll on which each one had written a prayerful message for my well-being. I was deeply touched by this, but as I couldn't answer them individually, I wrote the following to be pinned up in their classroom.

My young friends all in California
  seven thousand miles away,
Your prayers have weighed down the wings of angels
  on their way to my bed today.
They came in with the post and spilled about me
  like a mighty Host,
Each prayer a blossom, scented sweet as from a
  rosebush;
Yet their fragrance will not die
  but be pressed in life's page
And in my memory lie.

And now I send the angels back across the earth
To tell you what your prayers for me are worth:
Like jewels their kindness and concern shines bright;
Their sparkle dims my tear-filled sight.
And so, to each of you they carry this hope
That nothing will happen with which you cannot cope,
And that your life be free from fear,
And the light of your God will hover ever near
And guide you good and true.
This is the message, my dears, the angels bring
  from me to you.

ONE BIG
CONTRADICTION

This is Sunday morning again. Why do I harp on about Sundays? I don't like Sundays; never have, from those days when I was forced to attend Mass to those when I tried to conquer my fear of the wrath of God because I did not attend it.

God doesn't seem to trouble me so much in the middle of the week; but it is on a Sunday that my mind seems to start digging, probing, and unearthing all my faults; my good points never seem to stand out on a Sunday. I seem to be conscious of my mind more on a Sunday than at any other time because, there it is, arguing, always arguing some point or other, and whenever I think I've worked something out and the debate has gone in my favour, there's that voice that says, 'Well, that's your point of view. What about the other fellow's?' This is the worst of trying to see two sides of the coin at once, it never can be done, that's of course unless you hold it up to a mirror. Then again, your eyes, like your mind, must move from the front to the reflection.

I had some visitors yesterday and I was asked the old question, If I had the chance would I live this life over again? And my answer was, as always, a definite, 'No.' What would I alter? they asked. 'My face and my character,' I said. On further thought, however, I agreed to stick with my face but not with my character; I couldn't bear to live another life with anybody harbouring a character and make-up similar to my own, someone with this arguing, worrying brain, this debating brain that nearly always ends up in an intellectual mess, and this personality that's got to be subdued.

For here I am going over the Epilogues and my bits and pieces again today and I'm getting sick of them, together with my so-called poetry. I don't preach in them but I make definite statements about the philosophy I've gained from life . . . What philosophy? Where has all my reading got me – lying on the top of the bed feeling like nothing on God's earth on this Sunday morning knowing that I know nothing, really nothing.

They tell me I'm world famous. What does that mean? Damn all. They tell me I make people happy. Huh! Thousands and thousands of people have been made happy through reading my books; they write to me as if I were some kind of ancient philosopher. Do I see myself like this? *No*, of course not; more like a detector in an ailing body, a detector that has been given a capacity to pick out faults, foibles, pain and passion in others, and not forgetting myself.

. . . I think that's the trouble. I see myself as I really am, not as others see me. Who, I ask you, knows another person? Who? Nobody knows what goes on in another's mind. What we talk about are just things sliding off the surface, the depth is never touched except perhaps in madness.

IT IS SUNDAY. Whoever made Sunday? Well, not God: man made it. He made the seventh day the Sabbath or Day of Rest. But it is our first day. The Jews have their Sunday on a Saturday. When do the Mohammedans and all the other religious sects have their Sunday?

Well, there's one thing you can't alter: it's going to remain Sunday until twelve o'clock tonight and each minute's got to be used, so start working.

I sound a miserable so and so, don't I? And yet, I'm not, at least I never appear miserable to others. Tom says, 'That's one thing, you're never miserable.' Odd that. 'In the dumps at times, yes, blue, but you're not a miserable person. You couldn't be miserable because you see the funny side of things.' And that's true too. Hearing a funny line, reading a funny line, a quip on the wireless will send me off into laughter. I suppose that's Kate in me. For instance, the other morning I woke up feeling like nothing on earth. I was covered from head to foot in an allergy. I was going through the aftermath of another bleeding that had occurred the previous day, and on the wireless a man's voice was saying . . . I can't remember the exact words – but they were to the effect that he felt he was the only Jew in an Irish regiment stationed in Scotland. That was merely the gist of it, but I immediately saw the funny side of it. And Tom came hurriedly in, crying, 'Stop that! Now, stop that! You know what'll happen.' Yes, I knew what would happen. A good laugh or a good cry and my nose goes into action which so often necessitates an emergency trip into Newcastle.

How complex are we? How complex is a human being? I've said that nobody knows what is in another's mind. I've also said there was one place that no man had seen into, at least when alive, that is his own stomach. But the other day, just seconds before the laser was pushed down my throat, I thought that everything I'd ever thought had been in some way contradicted. I was one big contradiction, for here I was fearful of the very laser I had bought for this hospital being thrust down my gullet. Doctor Record's face was swimming above me: I felt drunk.

Would I come round?

God and Me

It's Sunday morning again.
I'm sitting up in bed;
God sits beside me
Shaking His head as He listens
To the voices on the channels,
Each panel stressing that the way to Him
Can be won – with guns in Ireland –
Only through His Son.

What a puzzle they set themselves, He says.
Jesus, Mohammed, Moses,
Crippin, Scargill, and your Tom,
I begot them all, every one,
And Flanders fields are strewn red
With those from My bed.

So Katie, woman of two syllables
As Priestland says,
What does your tiny grain of wisdom
For what it is worth bring forth?

Well, said I, for what it is worth
I think they have mistaken fear for faith,
So they suck up to Your Son,
And Prophets from all nations,
Those created by men long gone,
Intermediaries every one.

ONE BIG CONTRADICTION

Yes; yes, I see.
But think
That when you die and your mind dies with
*   you*
We may not meet as now,
When you are able to think I am near,
How then will you explain that faith is but
*   fear?*

Oh! that will be up to You;
If You are there to welcome me in,
Agnostic though I be,
I will then believe in what I see.

Oh, Katie, Katie, you are a fraud,
For why do you say when you would pray,
Lord, Lord, show me the way . . . why?
Come; come, get out of that bed,
We have work to do, both you and I.

But before we meet face to face
I will leave you a gift.
Hold it close, for it is My grace
And will put your agnosticism in its place.

Yet . . . being merely God,
I can but hope.

This Is My Prayer

Within the dark chaos of a troubled world
I will seek and find some Beauteous Thing.

From eyes grown dim with weeping will shine a
Light to guide me, and in Sorrow's Hour
I shall behold a great High Courage.

I shall find the wonder of an Infinite Patience,
and a quiet Faith in coming Joy and Peace.

And Love will I seek in the midst of Discord, and
find swift eager hands out-stretched in welcome.

I will seek Beauty all my days, and in my quest
I shall not be dismayed.

I SHALL FIND GOD

This poem is by Minnie Aumonier, author of *Gardens In Sun and Shade*.